THE PENGUIN CLASSICS

EDITED BY E. V. RIEU

L91

THE LITTLE FLOWERS OF

Saint Francis

WITH

FIVE CONSIDERATIONS ON THE
SACRED STIGMATA

*

Translated with an Introduction by
LEO SHERLEY-PRICE

PENGUIN BOOKS

Penguin Books Ltd, Harmondsworth, Middlesex
U.S.A.: Penguin Books Inc., 3300 Clipper Mill Road, Baltimore 11, Md
AUSTRALIA: Penguin Books Pty Ltd, 762 Whitehorse Road,
Mitcham, Victoria

—

This translation first published 1959

—

Made and printed in Great Britain
by Unwin Brothers Limited,
Woking and London

CONTENTS

Contents

Contents

FIVE CONSIDERATIONS ON THE HOLY STIGMATA OF SAINT FRANCIS

Contents

The Assisi Area

R. Arno

Verna
Bibbiena

Monte
Casale

S. Sepolcro

Arezzo

Città di
Castello

Gubbio

Cortona

Perugia

Assisi
Bastia · Carceri
S. Damiano
Lake
Trasimeno
S. Maria d'Angeli · Panzo
Rivotorto Spello
Cannara
Foligno

Sarteano

Trevi

R. Tiber · Todi

Spoleto

Orvieto

Terni
Narni · Poggio

Lake
Bolsena

Greccio

Orte
Rieti

Viterbo

Fonte Colombo

R. Tiber

INTRODUCTION

THE LITTLE FLOWERS OF SAINT FRANCIS
requires little introduction today, for, although it was not
translated into English until the middle of the last century,
it has long been one of the best-loved books in Christendom.
The work is not planned as a complete, chronological life
of the Saint, but gives us a series of intimate glimpses into
the life of Saint Francis and his early companions, and in so
doing recaptures something of the ardour and simplicity of
the friars in the spring-time of the Franciscan movement,
which was soon to take the world by storm. These scenes,
selected from the life of Saint Francis and his companions,
are arranged by the anonymous compilers into a Franciscan
anthology or bouquet, which has itself provided a title for
the work. But before discussing the contents of the *Fioretti*
itself, some mention should be made of earlier writings from
which much of its material is drawn.

SOURCES

The Three Companions

During the twenty years following the death of Saint
Francis, a considerable number of accounts were written
about incidents in his life, some of which were subsequently
lost or incorporated into later works. One of the earliest
surviving accounts is the *Story of the Three Companions* (*Legenda
Trium Sociorum*), traditionally ascribed to Friars Leo, Angelo,
and Ruffino. In the letter prefixed to this work, the writer
(or writers) say: 'We are not writing in the form of a Legend,
because for a considerable while Legends have been written
about his life and the miracles which God worked through
him. But just as from a fair field we pick certain flowers that
seem to us the most beautiful, so we do not follow an his-
torical sequence, but omit many events that have already

been clearly and accurately described in these Legends.' *The Story of the Three Companions* gives a simple, moving, and intimate account of Saint Francis and his first followers in the days when the virtues of poverty, humility, and joy in Christ shone so brightly, and such small and colourful details are given that there is no difficulty in recognizing that the scenes are described by one who took part in them. Here we are on firm ground, and are listening to an original disciple.

Thomas of Celano's Two Lives

Immediately after the canonization of Saint Francis, which took place in Assisi in 1228, Pope Gregory commissioned Friar Thomas of Celano – the reputed author of the Sequence *Dies Irae* – to compile a life of the Saint, and he may have indicated the general lines on which Thomas was to work. Although a competent writer, Thomas was not in a particularly good position to execute this task, for he had not entered the Order until 1215, and had spent much time outside Italy, so that he was not very intimate with Saint Francis and the inner circle of his disciples. Consequently Thomas's *Vita Prima*, written under the direction of the Pope and of Brother Elias, omits a great deal of interest and importance, and plays down the growing differences between the Spiritual party, who sought to uphold Saint Francis's Testament and ideals, and the 'modernist' party of Brother Elias, which sought to develop the Order on very different lines. As a result, the *Vita Prima* is incomplete and unsatisfactory; nevertheless, it remained useful for seventeen years, and won wide approval.

In 1244, Crescentius, Minister General of the Friars Minor, required all friars who had personal reminiscences of Saint Francis to record them and send them to Assisi, in order that a fuller life might be compiled. In response to this many friars sent in material, including the 'Three Companions', Leo, Angelo, and Ruffino, who sent in a number of *rotuli* from their retreat at Greccio, 'as well as Brother Philip, Brother Masseo, Brother Illuminato, and Brother John, companion of the revered Brother Giles and confidant of the holy Brother Bernard'. With this considerable authentic material at his disposal, Thomas set about to compile his *Vita Secunda*, either quoting directly from the writings themselves, or editing and rewriting material as seemed best. This he completed in 1247. The subsequent fate of most of these original documents is uncertain, and many are likely to have perished in 1266 when all writings not officially approved were ordered to be surrendered or destroyed. Many friaries and individuals, however, doubtless retained and concealed cherished MSS in defiance of this order. In particular we would like to know the fate of Brother Leo's vital *rotuli*, which were 'entrusted to the convent of Saint Clare [San Damiano] to be preserved for the instruction of posterity', and turned up some years later in the friars' library at Assisi. Father Delorme, in his edition of the Perugian MSS *Legenda antiqua S. Francisci*, holds that Brother Leo's writings survive in form in the latter part of this MSS, which somewhat resembles the well-known *Speculum Perfectionis*, itself long held to incorporate a considerable proportion of Leo's material.

Saint Bonaventura's Life of Saint Francis

Saint Bonaventura, the illustrious Minister General of the Order, and often regarded as its 'second founder', was requested by the Chapter General at Narbonne in 1260 to compile a definitive Life which would supersede all earlier and only partially satisfactory Lives. Making considerable use of Celano's work, Bonaventura compiled his *Legenda Major*, which although scholarly and accurate, is a formal hagiography on traditional lines, in which the vivid and lovable personality of the *Poverello* is transmuted into the conventional figure of a saintly founder of a great Order – the blueprint of a saint. It should, however, be remembered that the purpose of Bonaventura was not simply to write a history or record the memories of the Order's early days, for he had not known Saint Francis himself, but to justify the present policy of the Order and preserve its unity, now severely threatened by the growing divergence of view between the Spirituals and those who wished to see the Order administered like the earlier Orders, with its own buildings, endowments, libraries – a viewpoint excellent in its own way, but little resembling the life and teaching of the founder himself. This intention of Bonaventura, says Dr Moorman, was a right one, for 'a religious Order, like the Church itself, is a living organism, which must grow and develop . . . it is no good thinking that you can undo what has been done, nor stem the tide of progress. . . . Hence we see Saint Francis, the humble imitator of Christ, as the Saint, the wonder-worker, the founder of the most excellent community in the world.' (*Sources for the Life of S. Francis*, p. 148.) The Franciscan Order was indeed to grow rapidly, and from a small group of mendicant preachers, vowed to absolute poverty and simplicity, their sole Rule the Gospels, it had within fifty years of Saint Francis's death become a great power in Christendom, supported by Papal privileges, possessed of many buildings and endowments, and having in its ranks many great scholars and dignitaries. Great changes were, therefore, as inevitable as the transformation was startling. For Bonaventura it was therefore vital that, while the simple and lovely ideals of Saint Francis were to be cherished and made possible within the Order for ever, a wise and realistic administration must be ensured if decay and disintegration were to be prevented. Hence the somewhat formal tone of Bonaventura's own writing. He took considerable pains, however, to obtain first-hand evidence, and, as he tells us in the Prologue to his Life: '*Ut igitur vitae ipsius ad posteros transmittenda certius mihi constaret et clarius, ad eius locum originis, conversationis et transitus viri sancti, cum familiaribus eius adhuc supervirentibus collationem de his habui diligentem, et maxime cum quibusdam, qui sanctitatis eius et conscii fuerunt et sectatores praecipui, quibus propter agnitam veritatem probatamque virtutem fides est indubitabilis adhibenda.'*

The Actus Beati Francisci et Sociorum ejus

This work, probably compiled between 1322 and 1328, is the Latin MSS from which the greater part of the Fioretti is drawn, and is itself drawn from two earlier and distinct sources. The first section describes the lives of Saint Francis and his companions, while the second consists of a collection of stories about the friars of the Province of Ancona. The former group of stories clearly originates from the Spiritual party in the Order, and tells of its early days, emphasizes Francis's devotion to the ideals of poverty and simplicity, and gives accounts of his inner circle, Friars Bernard, Leo, Giles, Angelo, and Saint Clare. It has been suggested that behind this group of stories lies material provided by Brother James of Massa. Contrasting the two groups in the *Actus*, Paul Sabatier observes that in the first group 'the saints are real saints, already on their way to heaven, but they are still on earth: but . . . the friars of the March are different beings . . . bathed in a mysterious light and eternally rapt in contemplation'. And this second group manifestly originates from a later hand and a later generation of friars.

THE FIORETTI

The earliest MSS of the *Fioretti* itself is dated 1396, and is largely drawn and translated into Italian from this earlier Latin *Actus*. It is not the work of a single compiler, as the varying content and viewpoint of its chapters reveal. It is generally held that F. Ugolino da Santa Maria, who is quoted both in the *Actus* and *Fioretti* as the authority for a number of stories, played a considerable part in its compilation. F. Luke

Wadding, the well-known Irish seventeenth-century author of the *Annales Minorum* (1623), ascribes the entire work to him, and states that its original title was the *Floretum*. Paul Sabatier, on the other hand, expresses the now generally accepted view that F. Ugolino was not the author of all chapters, but made careful selection and use of various earlier sources, which he arranged and adapted without damaging their primitive simplicity and spirit. Accordingly, while the contents of the *Fioretti* vary considerably both in reliability and viewpoint, the life and personality of Saint Francis emerges so vividly and events have such an authentic ring that it is unquestionable that much of what we read today rests upon the testimony of friars of the first generation.

The date of the *Fioretti* remains uncertain, but the work probably originated in the March of Ancona, and has a particular interest in the lives of the friars of that Province, which was a stronghold of the Spiritual party in the Order, standing firmly for the literal observance of Saint Francis's Rule and Testament, and resisting the attempts of Friar Elias and his associates to compromise it and introduce ideas contrary to the expressed desires of the Founder. This viewpoint is reflected in several chapters (e.g. Chapter 47), where not only Elias but Saint Bonaventura himself are denounced as persecutors and apostates.

In its earliest form the *Fioretti* consisted of two parts: the *Fioretti* proper, containing fifty-three chapters, mainly drawn from the *Actus*; and five *Considerations on the Stigmata*, based on accounts in the *Actus*, the Lives of Celano and Saint Bonaventura, and other material, and drawn together with great skill and devotion by some unknown friar, probably from Tuscany. The chapters fall into two main sections: Chapters 1–37, Stories of Saint Francis and the early friars and Chapters 43–52, Lives of the Friars of the March of Ancona; with Chapters 38–42, Events in the lives of Saint Antony of Padua, Brother Simon of Assisi, and other friars, interposed between the above main sections. These fifty-two chapters are followed by the five *Considerations*, where the events leading up to the Stigmata and death of Saint Francis are described in considerable detail. It is held that the unknown compiler of the *Considerations* did not consider that the high mystery of the Stigmata had received sufficient attention in the *Actus*, and that he therefore omitted the relevant chapters of the *Actus* (9, 18, 39) and combined them with other material so as to give the subject proper treatment. The result of his work speaks for itself, for his moving, lovely, and graphic account enables the reader to make a spiritual pilgrimage to the lonely heights of La Verna, and to obtain a clear picture of the most Christ-like of all Saints, of whom Pope Pius XI said: 'Men have rightly hailed Saint Francis as "another Christ", because to his contemporaries, and to all future ages, he presented Christ living once again.'

SAINT FRANCIS

In an introduction it would be fruitless to attempt to survey the life of Saint Francis – the subject is too great and the background too wide to receive justice in a thumb-nail sketch – and those whose reading of the *Fioretti* makes them wish to study it further are advised to read a reliable modern work. Prominent among these are *The Life of S. Francis* by Father Cuthbert, O.S.F.C. (Longmans); *Saint Francis of Assisi* by O. Englebert, translated by E. Hutton (Burns Oates); and *Saint Francis of Assisi* by Dr J. R. H. Moorman (S.C.M. Press). To some readers, however, a few words about the spirit and aims of Saint Francis may be of help towards an understanding of the Saint and of the scenes so vividly recorded in the *Little Flowers*. This may, perhaps, be best prefaced by a quotation from his own *Praise of the Virtues* – virtues which are the foundations of Franciscan life:

Hail, O Wisdom, O Queen!
The Lord keep thee and thy sister holy and pure Simplicity.
Hail, O holy Lady Poverty!
The Lord keep thee and thy sister holy Humility!
Hail, O holy Lady Charity!
The Lord keep thee and thy sister holy Obedience.

The Apostle of Love

The whole life of Saint Francis radiates an active and limitless love of God and man. This love, springing from the inexhaustible love of the Godhead, 'stoops to conquer', and graven deep on Francis's heart were the words of his Master, *'The mark by which all men will know you for My disciples will be the love you bear one another'*. The life of Saint Francis illustrates that Christian charity embraces all things living, both man and beast, friend and foe, spending itself without counting the cost in that service which is the sure test and proof of love. Masseron writes: 'The seraphic love which is manifested towards God by devotion to the incarnate Word, under the triple form traditional in the Order of devotion to the Passion, devotion to the Eucharist, and devotion to the Virgin Mary, finds its most perfect expression towards one's neighbour in the apostolate. Saint Francis desired to save souls, as Christ Himself had saved them.' The charity of Saint Francis is no sentimental benevolence, but eminently practical and active, whether displayed towards God in worship and self-giving, or towards his fellow-men in serving their spiritual and material needs.

The Apostle of Joy

At heart Francis always remained the troubadour, the singer, the dramatic genius, who dedicated all his gifts to the glory and service of the Crucified. His constant meditation on the Passion of Christ and his sorrow for the sins of mankind, which had demanded the awful sacrifice of God's Son on Calvary, did not render Francis morbid and gloomy, but a man of joy. For while the mysteries of the Passion pierced him to the inmost soul, his sharing in them enabled him also to share the more profoundly in the joys of redemption won by the victorious and risen King of Glory. Therefore every hardship and rebuff, every pain of mind or body endured for Christ's sake brought him joy, and this he graphically illustrated to Friar Leo on their journey through the winter snow to Perugia (Chapter 7). In his first Rule he called for the spirit of joy among the brethren when he wrote (Chapter 7): 'Let the Friars beware of being sad and gloomy, like hypocrites; but let them show themselves *joyful in the Lord*, gay and pleasant.' And in all his writings Saint Francis's abiding delight in God and in His creation is nowhere more beautifully expressed than in his *Song of Brother Sun* (Appendix 3), composed during a time of great spiritual and physical suffering.

The Apostle of Humility

Francis had entered the service of Christ through the service of the lepers, the destitute, the 'under-privileged', the little people of small importance in the eyes of the world, but of infinite value to the heart of his Master, who had given a lasting example of humility and service in washing the feet of His own disciples, and by befriending 'publicans and sinners'. Francis, therefore, established the observance of Poverty as an essential note of his Order, and so as to foster the virtue of humility, 'he wished his brethren to be known as Minors, and the superiors of his Order to be called Ministers, so that he could use the very words of the Gospel that he had vowed to observe' (S. Bonaventura's *Life of S. Francis*, vi, 5). All friars were to be 'content with the lowest place', to prize humility and poverty above promotion and privilege, and to be 'little' among men. And it is due to the wisdom of Pope Innocent III that, when a majority of the Cardinals advised against the approval of Saint Francis's first Rule as being impracticable and visionary – an opinion at first held and later publicly retracted by Saint Dominic – the far-sighted Pope accepted the plea of Cardinal John of Saint Paul, who said: 'If we reject the petition of this poor man when he seeks approval for his evangelical way of life on the ground that it is an innovation or too hard to observe, let us beware lest we set ourselves up against the Gospel of Christ. For if anyone claims that to take a vow to observe the perfection of the Gospel is something novel, irrational, or impossible to perform, he is guilty of blasphemy against Christ, the Author of the Gospel' (Saint Bonaventura's *Life*, iii, 9). It is this eagerness of Saint Francis to render humble service to God and man, and to follow the road of simplicity and self-denial, that has remained a characteristic of the sons and daughters of Saint Francis to this day, and presents both a living witness to the truths of the Gospel, and a challenge to those Christians who are content to seek a comfortable compromise with the standards of the world.

The son of the Church

There have been superficial admirers of Saint Francis who seem to have imagined that he was either some kind of nature-mystic, or a rebel against the dogmas of the Church. But anyone who seeks the truth about Saint Francis with an open mind, studying the Saint's own writings and early Franciscan works, will be left in no doubt as to his unquestioning loyalty to the visible Body of Christ. Francis was clear-thinking and well instructed in his religion, with a firm grasp of the Faith; he was no vague sentimentalist or pious pantheist, and Nature which he loved so well spoke to him not of itself alone, but of the love and beauty of its Creator (see *The Mirror of Perfection*, 113). In all things, both living and inanimate, he saw the wisdom, power, and purpose of God. Of him might well have been written the lovely lines:

Introduction

I see His Blood upon the rose,
  And in the stars the glory of His eyes:
His Body gleams amid eternal snows,
  His tears fall from the skies.
All pathways by His feet are worn,
  His strong Heart stirs the ever-beating sea;
His crown of thorns is twined with every thorn,
  His Cross is every tree.

Yet Francis was not blind to the sins and abuses within the Church itself. Had not the crucifix in the little church of San Damiano bidden him, 'Restore My Church, which you see all in ruins'? Pope Innocent himself recognized its condition only too well, and welcomed Francis as a God-given source of new spirit and new faith. But, unlike many would-be reformers, Francis saw clearly that the weaknesses of the Church were of human origin, but that her nature and mission remained divine; she was the Bride of Christ, however discredited by her own children, and in her reposed the sole hope of man's salvation, both in this world and in the world to come. To abandon or reject the faith and fellowship of the Church would never have occurred to the mind of Saint Francis, whose mission was to serve Christ and to restore His Church from within, so that the fires of divine light and grace, so long obscured by the sins and errors of Christians, could shine forth in renewed glory. 'All the brethren shall be Catholics,' he wrote in his first Rule (§19), 'and shall live and speak as Catholics. If any shall have erred from the Catholic faith and life, either in word or act, and shall not repent, he is to be expelled from our Brotherhood.' It is, therefore, unmistakably clear that Saint Francis gave his whole love, loyalty, and obedience to the Church, seeking grace in her sacraments, and doing nothing without her guidance and blessing.

Anyone who may have tended to imagine that Saint Francis 'had no time for organized religion', or that his main interest

21

in life was in birds and beasts, will find his true character and beliefs revealed in the pages of the *Little Flowers*, as also in other early Franciscan writings. For men and women flocked to hear and follow him, not because he preached a 'popular', sentimental, emasculated version of the Christian Faith, but because they felt the magnetic attraction of one who lived the life of the Gospel literally and courageously. His purpose was not to make his hearers lovers of birds, beasts, and flowers, but to inspire them to follow Christ and make them lovers of the holy Cross. It was to teach them that, in the pattern of the crucified, they were to show love and courtesy to all God's creatures, not only to birds and beasts, but to the wicked, stupid, and unlovable among their fellow-men.

*

It is hoped that this translation, made from G. L. Passerini's edition of *I Fioretti del glorioso messere Santo Francesco e de' suoi Frati*, will provide a full, simple, and accurate version in modern English of one of the world's most delightful and moving classics.

LEO SHERLEY-PRICE

I.T.C. Royal Marines
Lympstone
Exmouth, Devon

These are the Little Flowers of the Glorious

SAINT FRANCIS

and his Friars

CHAPTER I: *How Saint Francis converted Master Bernard of Assisi*

FIRST of all, let us consider how the glorious Saint Francis resembled Christ in every action of his life. For as at the beginning of His ministry Christ chose twelve Apostles who were to renounce all worldly things and follow Him in poverty and all virtues, so when Saint Francis founded his Order, he chose twelve companions who took a vow of most noble poverty. And just as one of the Apostles incurred the judgement of God and finally hanged himself, similarly one of Saint Francis's twelve companions, named Brother John of Capella, apostasized and ended by hanging himself.

These things are a solemn warning to God's chosen, and should move them to humility and fear when they recall that no one is certain to persevere in God's grace to the end. And just as the holy Apostles were marvels of sanctity to the whole world, and were filled with the Holy Spirit, so these holy companions of Saint Francis were of such holiness that the world has never seen such wonderful and holy men since the time of the Apostles.

Like Saint Paul, one of them was caught up into the third heaven; this was Brother Giles. Another, Brother Philip Lungo, was touched on the lips by an angel with a burning coal, as was the prophet Isaiah. Another, Brother Silvester, spoke with God as friend to friend, in the same way as Moses. Another, by the purity of his understanding, soared up into the light of divine wisdom like that eagle, John the Evangelist; this was the very humble Brother Bernard, who was a very profound exponent of Holy Scripture. Another was sanctified by God and canonized in heaven while still living in the world; this was Brother Ruffino, a nobleman of Assisi. And, as will appear later, all of them were endowed with exceptional signs of holiness.

The first companion of Saint Francis was Brother Bernard

of Assisi, who was converted in the following way. When Saint Francis was still wearing secular clothes, although he had already renounced the world, he used to go about so unkempt and haggard as a result of his penances that many people thought him out of his mind. He was jeered at and driven away as a madman both by relations and strangers, who pelted him with stones and filth; but he bore all these injuries and insults with patience, as though he were deaf and dumb. Consequently Master Bernard of Assisi, who was one of the noblest, richest, and wisest men of that city, began to reflect deeply on Saint Francis's utter contempt for the world and his great patience in affliction; for although he had been hated and despised in this way by everyone for two years, he seemed more steadfast than ever. And Master Bernard said to himself: 'There can be no doubt that this man Francis has received great grace from God.' So he invited Saint Francis to dine and stay the night with him. And Saint Francis accepted, dining and lodging with him that night.

Then Master Bernard set his heart on seeing something of Saint Francis's holiness, so he had a bed prepared for him in his own room, where a lamp always burned throughout the night. But wishing to conceal his holiness, Saint Francis threw himself on his bed as soon as he entered the room, and pretended to sleep. After a short while Master Bernard did the same, and began to snore loudly as though fast asleep. So Saint Francis, thinking that Bernard was really asleep, rose from his bed early in the night and knelt down to pray, raising his eyes and hands to heaven, and exclaiming with great devotion and fervour: 'My God, my God.' And he continued with many tears until dawn, constantly repeating, 'My God', and nothing more.

As he uttered these words, Saint Francis was rapt in contemplation and wonder at the excellence of the Majesty of God, who had deigned to stoop to this world, and by means of His poor little servant Francis purposed to bring healing and salvation to his soul and the souls of others. Thus, enlightened by the spirit of prophecy, Francis foresaw the great things that God was about to do through himself and his Order. And when he considered his own inadequacy and lack of virtue he called upon God, and implored Him in His mercy and almighty power – without which human frailty is powerless – to assist and perfect all that he could not himself accomplish.

Now while Master Bernard watched Saint Francis's devotions by the light of the lamp, and considered the words that he uttered, he was touched by the Holy Spirit and inspired to amend his own way of life. So at dawn he called Saint Francis and said to him: 'Brother Francis, I am fully resolved in my heart to renounce the world, and to follow you in any way you direct.'

When Saint Francis heard this he was uplifted in spirit, and said: 'Master Bernard, what you tell me is so important and difficult a matter that we must ask guidance from our Lord Jesus Christ, and pray that He may be pleased to reveal His will in this thing, and show us how to put it into effect. So let us go together to the bishop's house, where there is a good priest, and ask him to say Mass. Then we will remain in prayer until Terce, and ask God to reveal the way He wishes us to choose by opening the missal three times.'

Master Bernard answered that he would be very glad to do this, so they set out and went to the bishop's house. And when they had heard Mass and continued in prayer until Terce, the priest took up the book at Francis's request, and making the sign of the Holy Cross, opened it three times in the Name of our Lord Jesus Christ. At the first opening, they found that passage in the Gospels where Christ said to the young man who asked Him about the way of perfection: 'If you wish to be perfect, go and sell all your possessions, and give to the poor ... and come, follow Me.'* At the second

* S. Matthew xix. 21.

opening they found the words of Christ to the Apostles when He sent them to preach: 'Take nothing for your journey, neither staff nor knapsack, shoes nor money,' wishing to teach them to trust entirely in God for their livelihood, and to devote their whole attention to preaching the holy Gospel. At the third opening of the missal they found Christ's words: 'If any man will come after Me, let him renounce self, take up his cross, and follow Me.'

Then Saint Francis said to Master Bernard: 'Here is the guidance that Christ is giving us. So go and carry out exactly what you have heard. And blessed be our Lord Jesus Christ, who has deigned to show us His way of the Gospel.'

When Master Bernard heard this, he went away and sold all his possessions – for he was very rich – and with great joy distributed everything among the poor, widows, orphans, pilgrims, clergy, and hospitals; and Saint Francis helped him to do this faithfully and wisely.

When a man named Silvester saw how Saint Francis was giving so much money to the poor, he was roused to avarice, and said to him: 'You did not pay me in full for the stone you bought from me to repair the church; so now you have some money, pay me.' Saint Francis was astonished at his greed, but being a true follower of the Gospel, he did not wish to dispute with him. So he thrust his hands into Bernard's purse, and with hands full of money, gave it to Silvester saying that if he asked for more, he should have it. But Silvester was satisfied and went home. In the evening, however, recalling what he had done that day, and pondering over the devotion of Master Bernard and the holiness of Saint Francis, he reproached himself for his avarice. That night, and the two following nights, he had a vision from God, in which he saw a golden cross issuing from the mouth of Saint Francis, the top of which reached up to heaven, and its arms extended from east to west. As a result of this vision he renounced all that he possessed for love of God and became a Friar Minor. And he attained such holiness and grace in the Order that he spoke with God as friend to friend, as Saint Francis was often to prove, and as will be told later.

Master Bernard likewise was so filled with the grace of God that he was often rapt in contemplation. And Saint Francis used to say of him that he deserved the greatest veneration, and that he was the true founder of the Order, because he was the first to renounce the world, keeping nothing for himself, but giving everything to Christ's poor; and that having entered on the way of evangelical poverty, he threw himself stripped of all things into the arms of the Crucified, to whom be blessing for ever and ever. Amen.

CHAPTER 2: *How Saint Francis went to talk with Brother Bernard*

SAINT FRANCIS, the devoted servant of the Crucified, as a result of his severe penance and constant weeping, had become nearly blind and could hardly see. On one occasion he left the place where he was and went to look for Brother Bernard in order to speak with him on the things of God. But when he arrived, he found that Brother Bernard was at prayer in a wood, and united to God in ecstasy. Then Saint Francis entered the wood and called to him: 'Come and talk with this blind man.'

But Brother Bernard who was a true contemplative, made no reply, for his mind was detached from the world and lifted up to God. And because, as Saint Francis had often proved, Brother Bernard had received an especial grace in speaking of God, he greatly desired to consult him.

After a short interval he called to him a second and third time in the same way, but Brother Bernard did not hear, and neither answered nor came to him. So Saint Francis went away somewhat disturbed, surprised, and inwardly grieved that Brother Bernard had not come to him although he had called three times. Turning back with these thoughts in mind, he had gone a short distance, when he said to his companion: 'Wait here for me,' and went to a secluded spot close by. There he began to pray, and asked God to reveal why Brother Bernard had not answered him. And as he prayed, there came a voice from God, saying: Poor little man, why are you so disturbed? Should a man leave God for a creature? When you called, Brother Bernard was united to Me, and that is why he could not come to you or answer you. Do not be surprised that he was unable to reply, for he was so detached in spirit that he did not hear anything that you said.'

When Saint Francis heard these words from God, he immediately hurried back to Brother Bernard in great sorrow to accuse himself most humbly before him of the wrongful thoughts that he had entertained. And when Brother Bernard saw him approaching, he hastened to meet him, and threw himself at his feet. Then Saint Francis begged him to rise, and very humbly confessed his thoughts and his distress, and told how God had answered his prayer. And he concluded: 'I command you under holy obedience to do what I tell you.'

Fearing that Saint Francis might order something extraordinary as he often did, Brother Bernard hoped to avoid this obedience in an honest way, and said: 'I am ready to obey you if you will also promise to do whatever I shall direct.'

When Saint Francis had given this promise, Brother Bernard said: 'Tell me then, father, what it is you want me to do.' And Saint Francis replied: 'I order you, under holy obedience, that when I lie down on the ground, you are to place one foot on my neck and the other on my mouth, and trample over me three times from one side to the other, reproaching and reviling me. And you are to say: "Lie there, boorish son of Pietro Bernadone! How can you be so proud, vile creature?" This is to punish my pride and hastiness of heart.

Hearing this, Brother Bernard did what Saint Francis directed under holy obedience as gently as he could, although he found it most distasteful. And afterwards Saint Francis said: 'Now order me to do what you wish, for I have promised you holy obedience.'

Brother Bernard said: 'I command you under holy obedience whenever we are in company, to rebuke and correct me severely for all my faults.'

Saint Francis was astonished at this, for Brother Bernard was a man of such holiness that he revered him greatly, and did not consider that he deserved any rebuke. And thenceforward Saint Francis avoided being with him too much because of this obedience, so that he would not have to utter any reproof to one whom he knew to be so saintly. But whenever he wished to see him, or to hear him speak of God, he used to leave him as soon as possible and go away. And it was wonderful to see the great love, reverence, and humility which Saint Francis the father showed toward Brother Bernard, the first-born of his sons, when he addressed him. *Praise and glory to Jesus Christ. Amen.*

CHAPTER 3: *How an angel came to the door to speak with Brother Elias*

IN the early days of the Order, when as yet there were few friars and no houses had been founded, Saint Francis made a pilgrimage of devotion to Saint James's* in Galicia, and took a few friars with him, one of whom was Brother Bernard. And as they were travelling together on this road, they found a poor sick man in a village by the way. Full of compassion for him, Saint Francis said to Brother Bernard: 'My son, I wish you to remain here and look after this sick man.' And Brother Bernard, kneeling humbly with bowed head, reverently

* The well-known shrine of Saint James at Compostella in Spain.

obeyed the father's command and remained there while Saint Francis and the other friars continued on their way to Saint James's. On their arrival, they spent the night in prayer in the Church of Saint James, where God revealed to Saint Francis that he would establish many friaries throughout the world, for his Order was to spread and grow into a great company of friars. And from then on, in fulfilment of this revelation, Saint Francis began to establish friaries in that country.

As Saint Francis was returning by the way he had come, he found Brother Bernard, and the sick man with whom he had left him restored to perfect health. So Saint Francis allowed Brother Bernard to visit Saint James's in the following year. Meanwhile Saint Francis returned to the Vale of Spoleto, where he, Brother Masseo, Brother Elias, and certain others dwelt in a remote place. And all were careful not to disturb Saint Francis in his prayers, both out of the veneration in which they held him, and because they knew that God revealed high matters to him during his prayer.

One day, while Saint Francis was at prayer in the wood, a handsome youth, dressed as a traveller, came to the door of the friary and knocked so impatiently, so loudly, and so long that the friars were startled at such an unusual way of knocking. Brother Masseo went and opened the door, saying to the youth: 'Where do you come from, my son? It seems that you have never been here before, since you knock in such an unusual way.'

'How, then, should one knock?' enquired the young man.

'Knock three times in succession,' said Brother Masseo; 'then wait for as long as a friar may take to say the *Our Father* and come to you. And if he does not come in that time, then knock again.'

The young man replied: 'I am in a great hurry; that is why I knocked so loudly. I have to go on a long journey, and I have come here to speak to Brother Francis; but since he is now in the wood rapt in contemplation, I don't want to disturb him. So go and send Brother Elias to me, for I hear that he is very learned, and I wish to put a question to him.'

So Brother Masseo went and asked Brother Elias to hurry to the youth; but he was offended, and refused to go. At this, Brother Masseo did not know what to do, or what to reply to the youth; for if he were to say, 'Brother Elias cannot come', he would be telling a lie, and were he to say that he was in a bad temper, he feared to expose a bad example. And while Brother Masseo was so slow in returning, the youth knocked again in the same manner as before. Brother Masseo returned to the door, and said, 'You have not knocked in the way I told you.' The young man replied: 'Brother Elias refuses to come to me. But go and tell Brother Francis that I have come to speak to him, and that since I do not wish to interrupt his prayer, ask him to send Brother Elias to me.'

Then Brother Masseo went to Saint Francis, who was at prayer in the wood with his face raised to heaven, and he gave him the young man's message and Brother Elias's reply. Now this young man was an angel of God in human form; and without changing his posture or lowering his face, Saint Francis said to Brother Masseo: 'Go and tell Brother Elias under obedience to go to the young man at once.'

When Brother Elias received Saint Francis's order, he went to the door in a great temper, threw it open very roughly and noisily, and said, 'What do you want?'

The young man answered: 'Friar, take care not to be as angry as you seem, for anger is very harmful to the soul, and prevents it from seeing the truth.'

Brother Elias said: 'Tell me, what do you want of me?'

The young man replied: 'I wish to ask you whether it is lawful for those who observe the holy Gospel to eat whatever is placed before them, as Christ told His disciples; and also whether it is lawful for any man to order things that are contrary to liberty of the Gospel.'

Brother Elias answered haughtily: 'I know about these things perfectly well, but I won't be questioned by you. Be off, and mind your own business.'

The young man said: 'I could answer this question better than you.'

At this Brother Elias slammed the door in a great rage and went off. Later he began to think over this question, and to have doubts about it, and he could not find an answer. For he was Vicar of the Order, and had framed and enacted a regulation, going beyond both the Gospel and the Rule of Saint Francis, that no friar of the Order might eat meat. And this question was therefore directed against himself.

Unable to quiet his mind, he recalled the modesty of the young man, and how he had told him that he could answer the question better than he. So Brother Elias went back to the door and opened it to consult the young man on this question; but he had already left, for Elias's pride rendered him unworthy to converse with angels.

Afterwards Saint Francis, to whom God had revealed the whole affair, returned from the wood and rebuked Brother Elias loudly and severely, saying: 'Proud Brother Elias, you have acted very wrongly, and have driven away the holy angels who come to guide us. I tell you, I am much afraid that your pride will cause you to end your days outside this Order.' And in due course it happened as Saint Francis had said, for Brother Elias did die outside the Order.

The same day, at the very hour in which the angel had left, he appeared in the same form to Brother Bernard, who was walking along the bank of a wide river on his way back from Saint James's. And he greeted him in his own language, saying: 'God give you peace, good friar.' Brother Bernard was surprised, and considering the young man's beauty, his knowledge of his own language, his greeting of peace, and his joyful face, he asked him, 'Where do you come from, good youth?'

'I come from the place where Saint Francis is living,' replied the angel. 'I went to speak with him, but I was unable to do so because he was in the wood contemplating the things of God, and I did not wish to disturb him. Brother Masseo, Brother Giles, and Brother Elias are living in the same house. Brother Masseo told me how to knock on the door in the way friars do, but Brother Elias, because he refused to answer a question I put to him, afterwards relented and wanted to hear and see me, but could not do so.'

The angel then said to Brother Bernard, 'Why don't you cross this river?'

Brother Bernard replied, 'Because I see that the water is deep, and fear danger.'

The angel said: 'Let us cross together. Don't be afraid.' And taking him by the hand, he transported him to the other side of the river in the twinkling of an eye. Then Brother Bernard realized that he was an angel of God, and with great reverence and joy, he exclaimed: 'Blessed angel of God, tell me your name!'

'Why do you ask my name, which is Wonderful?' answered the angel. With these words the angel vanished, and left Brother Bernard greatly comforted, so that he completed the entire journey with great happiness. And he noted the day and hour when the angel appeared.

On reaching the friary where Saint Francis was living with his companions, he gave them a full account of all that had taken place. Then they knew for certain that the same angel had appeared both to themselves and to him on the very same day and at the same hour, and they gave thanks to God.

CHAPTER 4: *How Brother Bernard established a friary at Bologna*

SINCE Saint Francis and his companions were called and chosen by God to bear the cross of Christ within their hearts, to display it in their actions, and to preach it with their tongues, they appeared – and indeed were – men crucified, both in their clothing, the austerity of their lives, and their doings, for they desired to bear shame and insult for the love of Christ rather than receive worldly honour, respect, or praise from men. Indeed, they took delight in insults and were embarrassed by respect; they went about the world as strangers and pilgrims, carrying with them nothing but Christ Crucified. And because they were true branches of the True Vine, which is Christ, they bore rich and plentiful fruit in the souls they won to God.

In the early days of the Order Saint Francis sent Brother Bernard to Bologna to bear fruit for God there, according to the grace that God had given him. And having signed himself with the sign of the cross, Brother Bernard set out under holy obedience and arrived in Bologna.

When the children saw him in a ragged, shabby habit, they jeered at him and abused him, thinking him a madman; but Brother Bernard bore all this patiently and gladly for the love of Christ. And in order to receive even worse treatment, he sat down openly in the market-place of the city. As he sat there a crowd of children and men gathered round him: one tugged at his cowl from behind, and another from in front; one threw dust at him, and another stones; one pushed him in this direction, and another in that. But Brother Bernard remained patient and unruffled, neither complaining nor moving away. And for several days he returned to the same place to endure similar treatment.

Since patience is evidence of perfection and proof of virtue, a wise doctor of laws, seeing Brother Bernard's great constancy and virtue, and considering how he remained undaunted by any ill-treatment and mockery during all these days, said to himself: 'It is impossible that this is not a holy man.' And coming up to him, he asked: 'Who are you, and why have you come here?'

In reply Brother Bernard put his hand into his breast, and drawing out the Rule of Saint Francis, gave it him to read. When he had read it and recognized its sublime counsel of perfection, he turned to his friends with the greatest wonder and admiration, saying: 'This is assuredly the highest form of the Religious Life of which I have ever heard. This man and his companions are the holiest men in the world, and whoever abuses him is the greatest of sinners, for he is the true friend of God and deserves the highest honour.'

And he said to Brother Bernard: 'If you need a place where you can serve God in a fitting manner, I will gladly provide it for the salvation of my soul.'

Brother Bernard answered: 'Sir, I believe that our Lord Jesus Christ has inspired you to make this offer, and I gladly accept it for the honour of Christ.'

So the judge led Brother Bernard to his house with great joy and affection, and gave him the promised house, which he prepared and furnished at his own expense. And thenceforward he acted like a father to him, and was the foremost protector of Brother Bernard and his companions.

Because of the holiness of his life, Brother Bernard began to be greatly revered by all the people, so that any who could see or touch him counted himself blessed. But, as a disciple of Christ and of the humble Saint Francis, Bernard feared lest the respect of this world might impede the peace and salvation of his soul. So he left the town and returned to Saint Francis, saying: 'Father, the friary has been established in Bologna. So send friars to occupy and maintain it, for I can do no good there; indeed, I fear to lose more than I could gain because of the excessive respect paid to me.'

When Saint Francis had received a full account of all that God had done through Brother Bernard, he gave thanks to Him who had begun to increase the poor little disciples of the Cross in this manner. And he sent some of his companions to Bologna and into Lombardy, where they established many friaries in various places.

CHAPTER 5: *How Saint Francis prayed about the temptations of Brother Bernard*

So great was the sanctity of Brother Bernard that Saint Francis held him in great reverence, and often spoke in his praise. One day when Saint Francis was devoutly at prayer, God revealed to him that Brother Bernard was about to endure many violent assaults by the devil. So Saint Francis, who had deep compassion for Brother Bernard and loved him as a son, prayed for him with tears for many days, commending him to Jesus Christ, that He would grant him victory over the devil.

And one day, while Saint Francis was praying fervently on this matter, God answered him, saying: 'Francis, have no fear, for all the temptations that Brother Bernard will have to face are a test of virtue and a means of winning the crown of merit. In the end he will overcome all his enemies, and his place in the Kingdom of Heaven is assured.'

At this promise, Saint Francis gave joyful thanks to God, and from that hour held Brother Bernard in even deeper affection and esteem. He showed this clearly not only during his lifetime, but also at his death. For when Saint Francis was about to die, surrounded like the patriarch Jacob by his devoted sons, all of whom were grief-stricken and in tears at being parted from so loving a father, he asked: 'Where is my first-born? Come near to me, my son, so that my soul may bless you before I die.'

Then Brother Bernard said in a low voice to Brother Elias, who was Vicar of the Order: 'Father, move to the Saint's right hand, so that he can bless you.' So Brother Elias came to his right hand, and Saint Francis, who had lost his sight through much weeping, laid his right hand on the head of Brother Elias, and said:

'This is not the head of my first-born, Brother Bernard.'

Then Brother Bernard came to his left side, and Saint Francis crossed his arms and placed his right hand on the head of Brother Bernard, and his left hand on the head of Brother Elias, saying to Brother Bernard: 'May God the Father of our Lord Jesus Christ bless you with every spiritual and heavenly blessing in Christ. You are the first-born, chosen in this holy Order to provide an evangelical pattern, and to follow Christ in the poverty of the Gospel. For not only did you give away all that you possessed and freely distributed everything to the poor for love of Christ, but you also offered yourself to God in this Order as a sacrifice of sweetness. Therefore receive the blessing of our Lord Jesus Christ, and of me, his poor little servant. May you be blessed with everlasting blessings, walking and standing, waking and sleeping, living and dying. Who ever blesses you shall be blessed, and whoever curses you shall not go unpunished. Be the first among your brethren, and let all the friars obey your instructions. Have authority to admit whom you will into this Order, and to expel whom you will. No brother is to exercise authority over you, and you shall be free to go or remain wherever you desire.'

After the death of Saint Francis, the friars loved and reverenced Brother Bernard as their venerable father. And when his death was drawing near, many friars came to him from different parts of the world, among whom was the angelic Brother Giles, who on seeing Brother Bernard said to him with great joy: '*Sursum corda!*' And holy Brother Bernard privately asked one of the friars to provide Brother

Giles with a place suitable for contemplation, and this was done.

When Brother Bernard reached his last hour, he asked that he be raised, and addressed the friars around him, saying: 'Dearest brothers, I do not wish to say much to you; but I wish you to bear in mind that you possess the same vocation in Religion that I have had, and one day you will come to the same condition as myself. And I know in my soul that I would not have renounced the service of our Lord Jesus Christ and of you to win a thousand worlds such as this. I beg you, my dearest brothers, to love one another.'

And after giving them other good counsel, he lay back on his bed, and his face shone with such indescribable joy that all the friars were amazed. And in this joy his most holy soul, crowned with glory, passed from this present life to the blessed life of the angels.

CHAPTER 6: *How Saint Francis passed Lent on an island in the Lake of Perugia, eating nothing but half a loaf*

SINCE Saint Francis, the venerable servant of Christ, was in some ways almost like another Christ given to the world for the salvation of the people, God the Father willed that in many of his actions he should conform to and resemble His Son Jesus Christ. This is shown in the venerable company of his twelve companions, in the wonderful mystery of the Stigmata,* and in the unbroken fast which he observed during the holy season of Lent in the following manner.

* The Stigmata were the sacred wounds of Jesus Christ, which were miraculously imprinted on the body of Saint Francis in the year 1224 on the Feast of the Holy Cross (14 September) during his retreat on Mount La Verna. This event is commemorated in the Church's Calendar on 17 September (the Feast of the Stigmata of Saint Francis). An account of this happening is given in the second Consideration; pages 152 ff.

One Carnival Day* Saint Francis had gone to the Lake of Perugia† to visit the home of one of his disciples where he was to spend the night, and there he was inspired by God to observe Lent on an island in the lake. So Saint Francis asked his friend for the love of Christ to take him out to an un-inhabited island in his little boat during the night of Ash Wednesday, so that no one should be aware of it. And because of the great devotion he bore Saint Francis, he took pains to carry out his request, and ferried him over to the island, Saint Francis taking nothing with him but two small loaves. And when they had reached the island, and his friend took leave of him to return home, Saint Francis earnestly requested him not to tell anyone where he was, and not to come back for him before Holy Thursday.

So the friend went away, and Saint Francis remained alone. And finding no building where he could shelter, he went into a very dense thicket where thorns and other bushes formed a kind of arbour or grotto, and here he spent the time in prayer and in contemplation of heavenly things. There he stayed throughout Lent eating and drinking nothing but half a small loaf, as his friend discovered on Holy Thursday when he returned for him, and found one of the two loaves and half of the other untouched. It is thought that Saint Francis consumed this out of reverence for the fast of Christ the Blessed, who fasted forty days and forty nights without taking any bodily sustenance. So by eating half of this loaf he avoided the venom of vainglory, and at the same time followed the example of Christ in fasting forty days and forty nights.

Afterwards, at this place where Saint Francis had observed such an amazing fast, God worked many miracles through his merits, so that people began to build houses and live there. And in a short time a fine large village was built there, as well as a house for the friars, which is known as the Friary of

* Shrove Tuesday.　　　　　　　† Lake Trasimeno.

the Island. And to this day the men and women of this place have a great reverence and respect for the spot where Saint Francis observed Lent.

CHAPTER 7: *Saint Francis writes that patience is the source of perfect joy*

ONE day Saint Francis was travelling from Perugia to Saint Mary of the Angels. It was winter, and he was suffering severely from the bitter cold. And he called to Brother Leo, who was walking a short distance ahead, saying:

'Brother Leo, although the Friars Minor throughout the land are setting a high example of holiness and edification, nevertheless write down and note well that this is not the source of perfect joy.' And a little further along the road Saint Francis called out a second time:

'Brother Leo, even though a Friar Minor could give sight to the blind, make the crooked straight, cast out devils, restore hearing to the deaf, make the lame walk and the dumb speak, and even raise to life one who had been dead four days, write down that this is not the source of perfect joy.'

And going on a little further, he cried out loudly: 'Brother Leo, were a Friar Minor to know every language and every science, and all the Scriptures, so that he could foretell and reveal not only the future but even the secrets of the conscience and soul, write down that this is not the source of perfect joy.'

Going on a little further, Saint Francis again called out loudly:

'Brother Leo, little lamb of God, even if a Friar Minor could speak with the tongue of an angel, know the courses of the stars and the properties of herbs; and if all the treasures of the earth were revealed to him, and he understood the ways of birds, fish, and all beasts, of men, of trees, of rocks, of roots, and of waters – write down that this is not the source of perfect joy.'

And walking on a little further, Saint Francis called out loudly:

'Brother Leo, even if a Friar Minor were such an eloquent preacher that he could convert all unbelievers to the Faith of Christ, write down that this is not the source of perfect joy.'

Saint Francis continued to discourse on this theme for nearly two miles, until Brother Leo in great bewilderment asked him: 'Father, I beg you in God's Name, tell me the source of perfect joy!'

And Saint Francis answered him: 'When we arrive at Saint Mary of the Angels soaked with rain, stiff with cold, covered with mud, and exhausted with hunger, and we knock at the friary door, and the porter asks angrily, "Who are you?" and we answer, "We are two of your brothers," and he says, "You are liars. You are a couple of rogues, who wander about deceiving folk and robbing the poor of alms. Be off with you!" and if he refuses to open, and forces us to stand outside all night in the snow and rain, hungry and frozen, then if we bear such ill-treatment, abuse, and dismissal patiently and calmly, without complaint, humbly and charitably thinking that the porter recognizes us for what we are, and that God moves him to denounce us; write down, Brother Leo, that here is the source of perfect joy.

'And if we go on knocking, and he comes out angrily and drives us away as importunate rogues with abuse and blows, saying, "Be off, you dirty thieves! Go to the poorhouse, for you're not going to eat or lodge here!"; and we bear this patiently, cheerfully, and charitably, Brother Leo, write down that here is the source of perfect joy.

'And if, driven by hunger, cold, and darkness, we continue to knock, begging him with tears to open and admit us for the love of God, and he, more furious than ever, says: "These are persistent rascals! I will give them what they deserve!"

and rushes out with a knotted stick, grabs us by our cowls, throws us to the ground, and rolls us in the snow, belabouring us with every knot on his stick; and if we bear this patiently and cheerfully, remembering the sufferings of Christ the Blessed, and how we should bear this for love of Him: Brother Leo, write down that here is the source of perfect joy.

'And now listen to the conclusion, Brother Leo. Above all graces and gifts of the Holy Spirit that Christ gives to His friends is the grace to conquer self, and willingly to bear any pain, injury, insult, and hardship for love of Christ. For we cannot glory in any other gifts of God except these, because they are not ours, but God's. Therefore the Apostle says: "What did you possess that was not given you by God? And if you have received it from Him, why do you glory as though you had it of yourself?" But in the cross of suffering and affliction we may glory, because this is our own. So the Apostle says: "I will not glory except in the Cross of our Lord Jesus Christ," to whom be everlasting honour and glory for ever and ever.'

CHAPTER 8: *How Saint Francis and Brother Leo recited Matins without a breviary*

ONE day, at the beginning of the Order, Saint Francis and Brother Leo were together in a place where there was no book from which to recite the Divine Office. So when the hour of Matins came, Saint Francis said to Brother Leo: 'Dearest brother, we have no breviary from which to say Matins, but in order that we may spend the time in the praises of God, I will speak and you shall reply as I tell you. I shall say: "O Brother Francis, you have done so much evil and committed so many sins in this world that you deserve hell." And you, Brother Leo, shall answer: "That is very true, and you deserve the deepest hell." '

And Brother Leo, with dove-like simplicity, replied: 'Willingly, Father; begin in God's Name.'

Then Saint Francis began to say: 'O Brother Francis, you have done so much evil and committed so many sins in this world that you deserve hell.'

And Brother Leo answered: 'God will work so much good through you that you will go to Paradise.'

'That is not what you are to say, Brother Leo,' said Saint Francis. 'But when I say: "O Brother Francis, you have sinned so greatly against God that you deserve to be cursed by God," then you are to say: "You certainly deserve to be numbered among the damned." '

And Brother Leo replied: 'Willingly, Father.'

Then Saint Francis beat his breast with many tears and sighs, saying in a loud voice: 'O my Lord, God of heaven and earth, I have committed so many sins and offences against You that I fully deserve to be under Your curse.'

And Brother Leo answered: 'O Brother Francis, God will do such things through you that you will be singularly blessed among the blessed.'

Saint Francis was amazed that Brother Leo always answered the opposite to what he had told him, and he rebuked him, saying, 'Why do you not answer as I told you? I order you under holy obedience to answer as I tell you. I shall say: "O Brother Francis, miserable little wretch, do you imagine that God will have mercy on you, seeing that you have committed so many sins against the Father of mercies and God of all comfort that you do not deserve to find mercy?" And you, Brother Leo, little sheep, shall reply: "You certainly don't deserve to find mercy." '

But when Saint Francis said: 'O Brother Francis, miserable little wretch, etc.', Brother Leo answered: 'God the Father, whose mercy is infinitely greater than your sins, will show great mercy on you, and will add much grace besides.'

At this answer Saint Francis, mildly annoyed and perturbed despite his patience said to Brother Leo: 'Why have you presumed to act contrary to holy obedience? And why have you so often answered the opposite to what I ordered you?'

Very humbly and respectfully Brother Leo replied: 'God knows, my father, that I fully intended answering as you ordered me; but God causes me to speak as He wills, and not as I intend.'

Saint Francis wondered greatly at this, and said to Brother Leo: 'I beg you most lovingly to answer me as I have told you this time.'

'Speak, in God's Name,' replied Brother Leo, 'and this time I will certainly answer as you wish.'

And Saint Francis, in tears, said: 'O Brother Francis, miserable little wretch, do you imagine that God will have mercy on you?'

Brother Leo answered: 'You will receive great grace from God, who will exalt and glorify you for ever, because he who humbles himself shall be exalted. And I cannot speak otherwise, for God is speaking through my mouth.'

And so, in this contest of humility, they kept vigil until dawn, with many tears and with great consolation of spirit.

CHAPTER 9: *How Brother Masseo tested Saint Francis*

SAINT FRANCIS was once staying at the friary of the Porziuncula* with Brother Masseo da Marignano, a man of great holiness, wisdom, and grace in speaking of God, for which reason Saint Francis had a great love for him.

* The Porziuncula (lit. 'the Little Portion') was an ancient little church in the woods below Assisi, dedicated to Saint Mary of the Angels, and belonging to the Abbey of Monte Subasio. Saint Francis and his companions were granted the use of this church by the Benedictines. Around it they built rough huts, and restored the church, then in disrepair (see *The Mirror of Perfection*, Chaps. 9, 10). Pope Honorius III, at the request of Saint Francis, granted a special indulgence to all who visited it.

One day Saint Francis was returning from prayer in the wood, and was just leaving it when Brother Masseo, wishing to put Saint Francis's humility to the test, went to meet him, and as though joking, said: 'Why after you? Why after you? Why after you?'

'What are you trying to say?' asked Saint Francis.

Brother Masseo said: 'I mean, why is it that the whole world is following you, and why does everybody want to see you, hear you, and obey you? You are not handsome, you are not very learned, and you are not of noble birth. Why, then, does the whole world want to follow you?'

When Saint Francis heard this, his heart was filled with joy, and raising his face to heaven, he remained a long time with his mind uplifted to God. After a while, returning to himself, he knelt down and gave praise and thanks to God. Then he turned to Brother Masseo in great fervour of spirit, and said: 'You want to know, "Why after me? Why after me? Why after me?" You want to know why the whole world is following me? This is granted me because the holy eyes of God most High, which observe both the good and the evil in every place, could not find among sinners anyone more vile, useless, and sinful than me, and because God could not find a viler creature on earth to employ for the marvellous work that He intends to accomplish. He has therefore chosen me to confound the nobility, the greatness, the power, the beauty, and the wisdom of the world. He has chosen me so that men may understand that every virtue and every good thing proceeds from Him alone, and not from any creature, and that no man may boast in His presence. But "he that glories, let him glory in the Lord", to whom belong all honour and glory for ever.'

Then Brother Masseo, receiving so humble an answer given with such sincerity, was filled with awe, and knew for certain that Saint Francis was grounded in true humility.

ONE day Saint Francis was walking along the road with Brother Masseo, and Brother Masseo had gone a short distance ahead. And reaching a place where three roads met, from which one could travel to Siena, Florence, and Arezzo, Brother Masseo asked: 'Father, which road should we take?'

'The road that God wills us to take,' replied Saint Francis.

'But how are we to learn God's will?' asked Brother Masseo.

'By the sign that I will show you,' replied Saint Francis. 'At this cross-roads where you are standing, I order you, by the merit of holy obedience, to spin round and round as children do, and you are not to stop turning until I tell you.'

So Brother Masseo began to spin round and round, and he turned for so long that he often fell to the ground out of giddiness. But as Saint Francis did not tell him to stop, and he wished to obey him faithfully, he rose and continued. At length, when he was spinning fast, Saint Francis cried: 'Stop still, and don't move!' And he stood still, and Saint Francis asked him: 'In what direction are you facing?'

'Towards Siena,' Brother Masseo replied.

'That is the road which God wants us to take,' said Saint Francis.

As they travelled along that road, Brother Masseo was very puzzled why Saint Francis had made him spin round and round like a child in front of layfolk passing by. But because of his veneration for the holy father he did not presume to mention this to him.

As they neared Siena, the townsfolk heard of the Saint's coming, and came out to meet him. And in their devotion to him, they picked up the Saint and his companion and carried them to the bishop's residence, so that they never set foot to the ground. Now at that very moment certain men of Siena were fighting one another, and two of them had already been killed. When Saint Francis arrived, he spoke to them with such devotion and holiness that he reconciled them to one another in complete peace, unity, and friendship. And when the Bishop of Siena learned of this holy action that Saint Francis had performed, he invited him to his house and entertained him with great honour that day and also that night. And on the following morning Saint Francis, who in true humility sought nothing but the glory of God in all that he did, rose early with his companion and left without the bishop being aware of it.

Because of this Brother Masseo complained to himself as he walked along, saying: 'What has this good man been up to now? He has made me spin round like a child, and now he has not uttered a single word or offered his thanks to the bishop who treated him with so much honour.' And it seemed to Brother Masseo that Saint Francis had behaved unwisely. But later, being enlightened by God, he reconsidered the matter, and reproached himself in his heart, saying: 'Brother Masseo, you are too proud, for you criticize the ways of God, and deserve hell for your senseless presumption. Yesterday Brother Francis accomplished such holy things that had they been done by an angel of God, they could not have been more wonderful. So if he orders you to throw stones, you should obey him; for what he has done on this journey has been the result of God's working, as has been shown in the good results that followed. For had he not reconciled those men who were fighting among themselves, not only would many have been slain by the dagger – and this bloodshed had already begun – but many souls would have been dragged down to hell by the devil. So you are very stupid and proud when you criticize events which are clearly in accordance with the will of God.'

Now all these things that Brother Masseo was considering in his heart as he walked along were made known to Saint

Francis by God. So Saint Francis came up to him and said: 'Hold firmly to these thoughts you were thinking just now, for they are good and profitable, and are inspired by God; but your earlier complaints were blind, vain, and proud, and were instigated by the devil.'

Then Brother Masseo clearly perceived that Saint Francis knew the secrets of his heart, and knew for certain that the spirit of divine wisdom guided the holy father in all that he did.

CHAPTER 11: *How Saint Francis wished to make Brother Masseo humble*

SAINT FRANCIS wished to make Brother Masseo humble, in order that the many gifts and graces given him by God might not fill him with vainglory, but that through the virtue of humility he might employ them to grow from virtue to virtue. So while he was living in a remote place with certain of his first companions – the truly holy friars, among whom was the said Brother Masseo – Saint Francis said to him one day in front of the whole company: 'Brother Masseo, all of your companions have the gift of contemplation and prayer, but you have the gift of preaching the word of God and edifying the people. So I wish you to undertake the offices of porter, treasurer, and cook, in order that these others may be free to devote themselves to contemplation. And while the other friars are at meals, you are to take your food outside the door of the friary; in this way you will be able to edify those who visit the friary with some helpful words about God before they knock, and no friar except yourself will have to go outside. And do this through the merit of holy obedience.'

Then Brother Masseo drew back his cowl and bowed his head, and he humbly accepted and performed these duties under holy obedience for many days, carrying out the duties of porter, treasurer, and cook.

But his companions, who were men enlightened by God, began to feel very uneasy in their hearts, knowing that Brother Masseo was a man of great perfection, equal to themselves or greater, and that all the burdens of the friary were being shouldered by him and not by them. Accordingly, moved by a single desire, they all went and begged the holy father that he would agree to share out these duties between them, since their consciences would not rest easy while Brother Masseo was carrying so great a burden.

Saint Francis listened to their advice, and agreeing to their request, called Brother Masseo, and said: 'Brother Masseo, your companions wish to share in the duties I have given you. So now I wish these offices to be divided.'

With great humility and patience, Brother Masseo answered: 'Father, whatever you command me to do, whether in whole or in part, I regard as the command of God.'

Then Saint Francis, seeing the love of the companions and the humility of Brother Masseo, gave a wonderful discourse on holy humility, showing that the greater the gifts and graces given us by God, the greater should be our humility; for without humility no virtue is acceptable to God. And after his talk he apportioned the offices between them with the deepest affection.

CHAPTER 12: *How on the road to France Saint Francis raised Brother Masseo into the air with his breath, and cast him to a distance*

OUR master Saint Francis, the wonderful servant and follower of Christ, wished in all things to conform perfectly to Christ who, according to the Gospel, sent out His disciples two by two into all the cities and places which He himself intended to visit. After His example, therefore, Saint Francis assembled twelve companions, and sent them out two by two to preach throughout the world. And in order to set them an example of true obedience, he first went out himself, following the example of Christ, who began with actions before teachings. So, having apportioned other parts of the world to his companions, he took Brother Masseo with him as his own companion, and set out on the road for France.

One day they arrived in a town famished, and in accordance with the Rule, went to beg bread for the love of God, Saint Francis going along one street and Brother Masseo along another. But because Saint Francis was undistinguished in appearance and short of stature, and was therefore considered a poor, miserable little man by those who did not know him, he collected nothing but a few morsels and crusts of dry bread. But Brother Masseo, who was a tall and handsome man, was given good large pieces and even whole loaves.

When they had ended begging, they met again outside the town to eat at a place where there was a beautiful spring, and beside it a fine broad rock, on which each laid the alms he had received. And when Saint Francis saw that the pieces of bread obtained by Brother Masseo were far better and larger than his own, he was filled with great joy, and said: 'O Brother Masseo, we are not worthy of so great a treasure!' And when he had repeated these words many times, Brother Masseo replied: 'Dearest father, how can one call this treasure, when we are so poor, and lack so many things that we need? We have no cloth, no knife, no dish, no bowl, no house, no table, and no man or woman to wait on us.'

The Saint Francis answered: 'And that is what I call a great treasure, where nothing has been provided by human labour, but everything has been given by divine Providence, as we can see clearly in the bread that we have collected, in this fair table of stone, and in this spring of clear water. So I would have us pray God that He will cause us to love with all our hearts this treasure of Holy Poverty, who is so noble that God Himself is her servant.'

So saying, when they had satisfied their bodily needs and offered prayer, they rose and continued on the road to France. And when they came to a church, Saint Francis said to his companion: 'Let us enter this church to pray.' And Saint Francis went behind the altar and began to pray, and during his prayer he was filled by the visitation of divine grace with such overpowering fervour that his soul was set on fire with love for Holy Poverty; his face glowed and his lips parted strangely as though he were emitting flames of fire. And coming thus aflame to his companion, he said to him: 'Ah, ah, ah, Brother Masseo; yield yourself to me.' He repeated these words three times, and at the third time Saint Francis raised Brother Masseo into the air with his breath and cast him a long spear's length from him. This astonished Brother Masseo, and he later told his companions that as he was raised and cast from Saint Francis by his breath, he had experienced such sweetness and consolation of the Holy Spirit that never in his life had he felt anything so wonderful.

After this, Saint Francis said: 'Dearest friend, let us now go to Saint Peter and Saint Paul, and ask them to teach us and help us to win the priceless treasure of most holy poverty, for it is so very noble and divine a treasure that we are not worthy to possess it in our worthless bodies. For this is the heavenly virtue by which all earthly and transitory things are trampled under foot, and by which every encumbrance is stripped from the soul, so that it may freely be united to the eternal God. This is the virtue which enables the soul, while still on earth, to enjoy fellowship with the angels in heaven; which went with Christ to the Cross; which was buried with Christ; which rose with Christ, and ascended with Him into heaven. And it is this virtue which also enables these souls who love it in this life to ascend into heaven, because it protects the weapons of true humility and charity. Let us therefore ask the most holy Apostles of Christ, who were perfect lovers of this pearl of the Gospel, to obtain this grace for us from our Lord Jesus Christ, that He, in His most holy compassion, will help us to become worthy to be true lovers, upholders, and humble disciples of this most precious, lovable, and angelic poverty.'

Conversing on these matters, they arrived in Rome and entered the church of Saint Peter. And Saint Francis began to pray in one part of the church, and Brother Masseo in another. And while Saint Francis continued long in prayer, with many tears and deep devotion, the most holy Apostles Peter and Paul appeared to him in great glory, and said: 'Since you ask and desire to observe that which Christ and the holy Apostles observed, our Lord Jesus Christ has sent us to tell you that your prayer has been heard, and that God grants you and your followers the perfect treasure of most holy poverty. And on His authority we promise that whoever, after your example, shall pursue this desire perfectly is assured of the blessedness of everlasting life. And both you and your followers shall be blessed by God.'

Having delivered their message, the Apostles vanished, leaving Saint Francis filled with consolation. And rising from prayer and rejoining his companion, he asked whether God had revealed anything to him; and he replied: 'No.' Then Saint Francis told him how the holy Apostles had appeared to him, and what they had revealed. And filled with joy on this account, they decided to return to the Vale of Spoleto, and to abandon their journey to France.

CHAPTER 13: *How Christ appeared to Saint Francis and his companions*

DURING the early days of the Order Saint Francis and his companions once gathered in a certain place to talk about

Christ. And in fervour of spirit he told one of them in the Name of God to open his mouth and speak of God as the Holy Spirit moved him. The friar obeyed, and spoke wonderfully of God until Saint Francis imposed silence upon him, and gave the same order to another friar. This brother also obeyed, and spoke of God with great penetration, until Saint Francis bade him also be silent. Then he ordered a third to speak of God, and he likewise began to speak so profoundly on the mysteries of God that Saint Francis knew clearly that he, like the other two, spoke by the Holy Spirit.

This was confirmed by an unmistakable sign, for, as they were conversing in this way, Christ the Blessed appeared in the midst of them in the form of a most beautiful youth. And He blessed them all, and filled them with such sweetness that they all entered into rapture, and lay as though dead, insensible to all worldly things.

And when they returned to themselves, Saint Francis said to them: 'My dearest brothers, give thanks to God, who has willed to reveal the treasures of divine wisdom through the lips of the simple; for it is God who opens the mouths of the dumb, and makes the tongues of the simple to speak with great wisdom.'

CHAPTER 14: *How the people of Assisi ran to Saint Mary of the Angels to extinguish the fire*

WHEN Saint Francis stayed in Assisi, he often visited Saint Clare and gave her spiritual counsel. Now she had a great wish to eat a single meal with him, and had asked him many times to do so, but he was never willing to grant her this favour. When his companions learned of Saint Clare's wish, they said to Saint Francis: 'Father, it seems to us that such strictness does not accord with divine charity, if you refuse to grant Sister Clare, a virgin so holy and beloved by God, such a trifling request as to eat with you, and especially since it was through your preaching that she abandoned the riches and pomp of the world. Indeed, had she asked a greater favour than this, you should grant it her, for she is your spiritual plant.'

Saint Francis answered: 'Do you think that I should grant her request?'

The companions said: 'Yes, Father, it is fitting that you should grant her this favour.'

Then Saint Francis said: 'Since it seems fitting to you, I consent. But to give her greater pleasure, I would like the meal to take place in Saint Mary of the Angels, for she has been a long while enclosed in San Damiano,* and it will give her pleasure to see the friary of Saint Mary's again for a short while, since it was there that her hair was shorn, and she became the bride of Christ. We will eat together there in the Name of God.'

On the appointed day, Saint Clare left her convent with a single companion, and escorted by the companions of Saint Francis, arrived at Saint Mary of the Angels. And when she had reverently offered her devotions to the Virgin Mary before her altar, where she had been shorn and veiled, they showed her around the friary until it was time for the meal.

Meanwhile Saint Francis had ordered the table to be set on the bare ground, as was his custom. And when the time came for dinner, Saint Francis and Saint Clare sat down together, and one of the companions of Saint Francis with the companion of Saint Clare, and then all the other companions humbly took their places at table.

During the first dish, Saint Francis began to discourse on God so sweetly and so wonderfully that the richness of

* The ancient church which was the scene of Saint Francis's conversion, where he heard the crucifix say to him, 'Francis, go and repair My church, which, as you see, is wholly in ruins' (II Celano, Chap. 6). It was to become the mother-house of the Second Order of Saint Francis, under Saint Clare.

divine grace descended upon them, and they were all rapt in God. And while they were in this state of rapture, with their eyes and hands raised to heaven, the folk of Assisi, Bettona, and the surrounding countryside saw Saint Mary of the Angels, the whole friary and the wood around it ablaze with light, as though a great fire were consuming the church, the friary, and the wood together. So the men of Assisi, convinced that everything was in flames, ran down in great haste to put out the fire. But when they arrived at the friary and found nothing burning, they entered and found Saint Francis with Saint Clare and all their companions seated around that humble table rapt in contemplation of God. Then they realized that it had been a heavenly and not an earthly fire which God had miraculously caused to appear in order to display and represent the fire of divine love which burned in the souls of these holy friars and nuns. And they went away greatly edified.

After a long while Saint Francis, Saint Clare, and their companions returned to themselves, and feeling much refreshed by spiritual nourishment, had little desire for bodily food. So when this blessed meal was ended, Saint Clare, honourably escorted, returned to San Damiano.

When they saw her, the sisters were very glad, because they had feared that Saint Francis might have sent her away to rule over some other convent, as he had already sent her own sister, the holy Agnes, to rule as abbess over the convent of Monticelli in Florence. For Saint Francis had once said to Saint Clare: 'Be ready in case it is necessary for me to send you elsewhere.' And being a daughter of holy obedience, she had answered: 'Father, I am always ready to go wherever you may send me.' So the sisters were delighted to welcome her back once more, and thenceforward Saint Clare remained there greatly consoled.

A SHORT while after his conversion Saint Francis, the humble servant of Christ, having already gathered many companions and received them into the Order, was in great perplexity as to what he ought to do; whether to devote himself wholly to prayer, or whether to preach from time to time. And he greatly desired to know God's will in the matter. But because his humility was so profound that it would not permit him to rely on his own judgement or his own prayers, he wished to learn God's will through the prayers of others. So he called Brother Masseo and said: 'Go to Sister Clare, and ask her on my behalf to pray earnestly with some of the most spiritual of her companions that God may be pleased to show me which way is best; whether to devote myself to preaching, or wholly to prayer. Then go to Brother Silvester, and ask him to do the same.'

Now in the world this friar had been Master Silvester, the same who had seen issuing from the mouth of Saint Francis a cross of gold which reached as high as heaven and extended to the ends of the earth. And Brother Silvester was a man of such holiness that whatever he sought from God was granted, and he often conversed with God, so that Saint Francis had a great veneration for him.

So Brother Masseo went in accordance with Saint Francis's instructions, and took his message first to Saint Clare and then to Brother Silvester. And as soon as Brother Silvester had received it, he entered into prayer, and during his prayer he received God's answer. Then he called Brother Masseo and said to him: 'This is God's message which you are to deliver to Brother Francis: "God has not called him to this state solely for his own salvation, but in order that he may gather in a harvest of souls, and that many may be saved through him." '

Having received this answer, Brother Masseo went to Saint Clare to learn what guidance she had received from God, and she replied that she and her companions had received the same answer from God as Brother Silvester. So Brother Masseo returned with this answer to Saint Francis, who welcomed him with the greatest love, washing his feet and preparing a meal for him. And when he had eaten, Saint Francis called Brother Masseo into the wood, and knelt down before him. And he drew back his cowl, and folding his arms in the form of a cross, he asked: 'What is the command of my Lord Jesus Christ?'

Brother Masseo answered: 'Christ has given an answer both to Brother Silvester and to Sister Clare and her sisters, and has revealed that it is His will that you should go and preach throughout the world, because He has not chosen you for yourself alone, but for the salvation of others as well.'

When Saint Francis had heard this answer, and knew it to be the will of Christ, he rose with very great fervour and said: 'Let us go forth in the Name of God!' He took with him as companions Brother Masseo and Brother Angelo, both holy men, and set out with burning zeal regardless of road or path, and came to a fortress-town called Cannara. There Saint Francis began to preach, having first ordered the swallows to cease twittering and keep silence until he had ended his sermon; and the swallows obeyed him. He preached there with such ardour that the men and women of the town were all so moved that they wished to follow him and leave their homes. But Saint Francis would not allow this, saying: 'Don't be in a hurry, and don't leave here: I will explain what you must do for the salvation of your souls.' It was then that he decided to establish the Third Order, for the universal salvation of all people. So leaving them much consoled and well disposed to penitence, he went on to a place between Armano and Bevagno.

Continuing on his way in the same fervour, he raised his eyes and saw by the roadside some trees, on which rested an innumerable flock of birds. Saint Francis was filled with wonder at this, and said to his companion: 'Wait here for me on the road, and I will go and preach to my sisters the birds.' And he went into the field and began to preach to the birds that were on the ground, and immediately those in the trees flew down to him. And they all remained motionless until Saint Francis had ended his preaching, and even then did not depart until he had given them his blessing. And as Brother Masseo afterwards told Brother Jacomo da Massa, even when Saint Francis walked among them and touched them with his cloak, not one of them stirred.

The substance of Saint Francis's sermon was this: 'My little sisters the birds, you have received many things from God your Maker, and you should praise Him everywhere, for He has clothed you with double and triple plumage, and given you freedom to fly wherever you will. He has preserved your species in the ark of Noah, so that it should not perish out of the world. Again, you owe to Him the element of the air, which He has assigned to you. Furthermore, you do not sow or reap, yet God feeds you and gives you the rivers and springs to drink from, the mountains and hills for your refuge, and the high trees in which to build your nests. And although you do not know how to spin or sew, God clothes both you and your young. Your Creator shows great love for you, since He has given you so many blessings. So, my little sisters, keep yourselves from the sin of ingratitude, and always strive to praise God.'

As Saint Francis was speaking to them, all the birds began to open their beaks, stretch out their necks, and reverently bow their heads to the ground, showing by their actions and songs that the words of the holy father gave them the greatest delight. And Saint Francis was glad and rejoiced with them, filled with wonder at so great a host of birds, their beauty

and variety, their attention to him, and their tameness. And
he devoutly praised the Creator in them for all these things.

When at length he had ended his discourse, Saint Francis
made the sign of the cross over them and gave them leave to
depart. Whereupon all the birds rose into the air in a body
with wonderful song. Then they formed themselves into four
flights in the form of the cross which Saint Francis had made
over them; one flight travelled towards the east, another to
the west, the third to the south, and the fourth to the north.
And as it went, each flight sang wonderfully, signifying in this
way that as Saint Francis, the standard-bearer of the cross of
Christ, had preached to them and made the sign of the cross
over them, so that they dispersed to the four quarters of the
world, so the preaching of the cross of Christ, renewed by
Saint Francis, would be borne by him and his friars throughout the whole world. And these friars, like the birds, would
possess nothing of their own, but entrust their lives solely
to the providence of God.

CHAPTER 16: *How a little boy fell unconscious when he saw
Saint Francis talking with Christ*

DURING the lifetime of Saint Francis a very pure and
innocent boy was received into the Order, and lived in a
friary so small that necessity obliged the friars to sleep two
in a bed. One day Saint Francis visited this friary, and in the
evening after Compline he lay down to rest, so that he could
rise to pray during the night as was his custom. The little
boy had set his heart on closely observing the life of Saint
Francis, and particularly wished to discover what he did when
he got up during the night. So lest sleep should overcome
him, when he lay down to sleep beside Saint Francis, the boy
knotted his own cord to that of Saint Francis, so that he
would feel when he rose. Saint Francis did not notice this, but

during the early part of the night when all the friars were asleep, Saint Francis rose and found his cord fastened in this way. And freeing it so gently that the boy did not wake, he went out alone into a wood that was close to the friary, where he entered a little cell standing there and began to pray.

After some while the boy awoke, and finding his cord unfastened and Saint Francis gone, he got up and went to look for him. And finding the gate that led into the wood standing open, he guessed that Saint Francis had gone there, and went into the wood. As he drew near the place where Saint Francis was at prayer, he began to hear the sound of voices, and came closer to see and discover what he heard. And he saw Saint Francis encircled by a wonderful light, in which were Christ and the Virgin Mary, Saint John the Baptist, Saint John the Evangelist, and a countless host of angels, who were speaking with Saint Francis.

At this sight and sound the boy fell senseless to the ground. And when the mystery of this holy vision came to an end, Saint Francis on his way back to the friary stumbled against the boy who was lying on the ground as though lifeless. He lifted him in his arms with compassion and carried him to bed, as the good shepherd carries his sheep. And later, learning from him how he had seen the vision, he ordered him not to tell anyone about it during his lifetime. Subsequently the boy grew up in the great grace of God and in devotion to Saint Francis, and became a leading figure in the Order. And only after the death of Saint Francis did he reveal this vision to the friars.

CHAPTER 17: *How Saint Francis held a General Chapter at Assisi*

SAINT FRANCIS, the faithful servant of Christ, once held a Chapter at Saint Mary of the Angels, for which over five thousand friars assembled. It was also attended by Saint Dominic, head and founder of the Order of Friar Preachers, who was on his way from Burgundy to Rome. And hearing of the General Chapter that Saint Francis had summoned in the plain around Saint Mary of the Angels, he came to see it with seven friars of his Order. Also present at this Chapter was a Cardinal who was deeply attached to Saint Francis, and to whom Saint Francis had foretold that he would become Pope; and this later came to pass.* This Cardinal had come specially to Assisi from Perugia, where the Papal Court was then in residence, and came daily to visit Saint Francis and his friars. On some days he sang the Mass, and on others he addressed the friars in Chapter; and whenever he came to visit that holy assembly the Cardinal was filled with the greatest comfort and joy. And looking at the friars seated in the plain around Saint Mary's, company by company, some forty strong, some a hundred, others two hundred or three hundred, all of them entirely occupied in spiritual discussion, in prayer, in tears, or in acts of charity, and all conducting themselves with such quietness and restraint that no discord ever arose, he was amazed that so vast a gathering could be so orderly. And he said with tears and great devotion: 'This is indeed the camp and army of the knights of God.'

No idle chatter or foolish joking were to be heard throughout this vast assembly, but wherever a company of friars gathered, they either prayed, recited the Office, did penance for their own sins and those of their benefactors, or spoke of the salvation of souls.

The camp consisted of shelters made of wicker hurdles and rush mats, set up in groups corresponding to the provinces to which the friars belonged, and for this reason the Chapter

---

* Cardinal Ugolino, Bishop of Ostia, a prelate greatly devoted to Saint Francis, and his patron at the Roman Curia. At Saint Francis's request Pope Innocent appointed him Protector of the Order. He later became Pope Gregory IX.

became known as the Chapter of hurdles or mats. The friars slept on the bare ground, and some had a little straw; their pillows were stones or logs. Because of this, so deep was the respect of whoever heard of or saw them, and so great was the fame of their holiness that many Counts, Barons, Knights, and other nobles and many priests, Cardinals, Bishops, Abbots, and other clergy came from the Papal Court which was then at Perugia, and from other parts of the Vale of Spoleto, in order to see so holy, numerous, and humble an assembly, containing so many saintly men, the like of which the world have never seen. And chiefly they came to see the head and most holy father of these holy men, who had robbed the world of so noble a prey, and gathered so excellent and devout a flock to follow in the footsteps of the True Shepherd, Jesus Christ.

When the General Chapter had assembled, Saint Francis, the holy father and Minister General of them all, expounded the word of God in great fervour of spirit, and addressed them in a loud voice as the Spirit of God moved him to speak. For the theme of his sermon he chose the words: 'My little children, we have promised great things to God, but He has made even greater promises to us if we will keep our word, and look forward with faith to the fulfilment of His promises. The pleasures of this world are short-lived, but the pain that follows them is everlasting. The pain of this world is insignificant, but the glory of the life to come is infinite!' And he preached on these words with great devotion, encouraging the friars, and urging them to obey and reverence Holy Mother Church, to maintain brotherly charity, to worship God on behalf of all mankind, to be patient in wordly adversity and modest in prosperity. They were to keep themselves pure and chaste as the angels, to live in peace and harmony with God and with men, to preserve a quiet conscience, and to love and observe holy poverty. Then he said: 'I command all of you assembled here, by the virtue of holy obedience, that none of you are to worry about food, drink, or any bodily needs. Your sole task is to pray, and to praise God. Leave all concern for your bodily needs to Him, for He has made you His especial care.' And all the friars received this command with joyful hearts and happy faces. And when Saint Francis had ended his address, they all knelt in prayer.

Saint Dominic, who was present at all these proceedings, was startled at Saint Francis's command, and considered it rash, for he could not imagine how such a great number could be administered without any care or provision for its bodily needs. But the Chief Shepherd, Christ the Blessed, willed to show that He cares for His sheep, and has an especial love for His poor. And forthwith He inspired the people of Perugia, Spoleto, Foligno, Spello, Assisi, and all the surrounding districts to bring food and drink for this holy assembly. And men suddenly arrived from those places with donkeys, horses, and carts laden with bread and wine, beans, cheese, and other good things to eat to meet the needs of these poor men of Christ. In addition, they brought table linen, pots, bowls, cups, and other vessels necessary for so great a number. And whoever could bring the most or serve most busily counted himself blessed, so that even Knights, Barons, and other nobles who had come to see the friars remained to serve them with great humility and respect.

When Saint Dominic saw these things, and recognized that divine providence was clearly responsible for them, he humbly acknowledged that he had misjudged Saint Francis in thinking his command ill-considered. And he knelt down before him, humbly confessing his fault, and adding: 'God has clearly an especial care for these poor and holy men, and I did not realize it. Henceforward I promise to observe evangelical poverty myself, and in God's name I denounce all brothers of my Order who shall presume to possess anything of their own.' So Saint Dominic was much edified by the faith of the most holy Francis, by the obedience and poverty of so great and disciplined a company, and by the generous abundance of every good thing supplied by the providence of God.

During this Chapter Saint Francis was told that many of the friars were wearing iron corselets and pieces of mail next the body, which made many of them ill and brought some near to death, so that they were unable to pray properly. So Saint Francis, as a wise father, ordered under holy obedience all who wore these corselets or pieces of mail to remove them and lay them down before him. And when this had been done, at least five hundred corselets were counted, and many more pieces of mail both for arms and stomach, so that they formed a great pile; and Saint Francis ordered them to be left there.

When the Chapter had ended, Saint Francis encouraged them all to do good, and told them how to preserve themselves from sin in this wicked world. And he dismissed them to their own Provinces filled with spiritual joy, and fortified by God's blessing and his own.

CHAPTER 18 : *How Christ appeared to Saint Francis when he was suffering from a disease of the eyes*

AT one time, when Saint Francis had a grave disease of the eyes, Cardinal Ugolino, the Cardinal-Protector of the Order, who had a great love for him, sent a letter inviting him to visit him at Rieti, where the best eye-physicians lived. When Saint Francis received the Cardinal's letter, he went first to San Damiano to give counsel to Saint Clare, the most devout spouse of Christ, intending to go on to the Cardinal. But during the night after his arrival Saint Francis's eyes became so much worse that he could not see the light at all. Accordingly, since he could not continue his journey, Saint Clare made a little cell of reeds so that he could rest more comfortably. But, troubled both by the pain of his disease and by swarms of mice which caused him great inconvenience, Saint Francis could obtain no rest, either by day or by night. And as he endured increasing distress, he began to think and became convinced that this was a punishment from God for his sins. And he began to thank God with his whole heart and with his lips, and cried in a loud voice: 'My Lord, I deserve this and far worse. My Lord Jesus Christ, Good Shepherd, who hast shown Thy mercy toward us unworthy sinners by many pains and bodily anguish; grant me, Thy little sheep, such grace and virtue that no sickness, pain, or distress may cause me to fall from Thee.'

And as he prayed, there came a voice from heaven, saying: 'Francis, answer Me: If all the world were gold, and all the mountains, hills, and rocks were precious stones, and all the seas, rivers, and springs were balm, and you were to discover another treasure far more precious than all these things, just as gold is more precious than earth, balm than water, and precious stones than mountains and rocks; and if this greater treasure were to be given you as a result of this infirmity, would you not be well content and very happy?'

Saint Francis answered: 'Lord, I do not deserve so precious a treasure.'

And the voice of God said to him: 'Rejoice, Francis, for this is the treasure of everlasting life which I reserve for you until the hour when I shall bestow it upon you. And this sickness and affliction is the pledge of that blessed treasure.'

Then Saint Francis, filled with sublime joy at so glorious a promise, called his companion and said: 'Let us go to the Cardinal.' And having first comforted Saint Clare with holy words, he humbly took leave of her and set out for Rieti.

As he approached the city, so great a crowd of people came out to meet him that he decided not to enter, but went into a church standing about two miles distant. But when the townsfolk learned that he was in the church, they poured out to see him in such numbers that the vineyard belonging to the church was ruined and all the grapes were picked. As a result the priest was inwardly very distressed, and regretted that he had invited Saint Francis into his church. But God revealed the thoughts of the priest to Saint Francis, and he called for him and said:

'Dearest Father, how many measures of wine does this vineyard yield when it is at its best?'

'Twelve measures,' he replied.

'I beg you, Father, bear with me patiently,' said Saint Francis, 'and let me stay here a few days, because I find it very restful. And for the love of God and of me, His poor little man, give everyone leave to pick grapes in your vineyard. I promise you, in the name of my Lord Jesus Christ, that it shall yield you twenty measures each year.' And during his stay there, Saint Francis gathered a great harvest of souls among the folk who came to visit him, many of whom went away burning with the love of God, and renounced the world.

Trusting in Saint Francis's promise, the priest allowed free use of the vineyard to all who visited him. Marvellous to tell, the vineyard was completely stripped, so that hardly any grapes were left to gather. But at vintage-time the priest picked the few remaining bunches, put them in the vat, and pressed them; and he obtained twenty measures of the best wine, as Saint Francis had promised.

This miracle was clearly intended to show that, as the vineyard stripped of its grapes yielded abundant wine through the merits of Saint Francis, so Christian people barren of virtue, through sin, often yield the good fruit of penitence in abundance through the merits and teaching of Saint Francis.

CHAPTER 19 : *How a Novice was tempted to abandon the Rule*

A YOUNG man of noble family and accustomed to luxury entered the Order of Saint Francis, and from that day, at the instigation of the devil, he began to conceive such a loathing for the habit he wore that he felt as though he was wearing a filthy sack. He had a horror of the sleeves, he detested the hood, and the length and roughness of the robe seemed an intolerable affliction. And becoming increasingly discontented in the Religious Life, he at length decided to renounce the habit and return to the world.

Now this friar, as he had been instructed by his Novice-Master, already observed the custom of passing hourly before the altar of the friary, where the Body of Christ reposed, genuflecting with great reverence, and prostrating himself with the cowl drawn back and the arms crossed. And on the night when he was intending to leave, he chanced to pass before the altar of the friary, and as he did so, he genuflected and paid reverence in accordance with the custom. Suddenly he was rapt in spirit, and God showed him a wonderful vision, in which he saw a countless host of Saints pass before him, as though in a procession. They walked two by two, and all of them were clothed in very beautiful and precious robes; their faces and hands shone like the sun, and they moved to the hymns and songs of the angels. Among these Saints were two men even more richly robed and adorned than the others. These were encircled by a radiance so brilliant that those who saw them were filled with amazement. And at the rear of the procession he saw another, adorned with such glory that he seemed like a newly-invested knight, honoured above all the others.

As the young man watched this wonderful vision, he was filled with amazement, and did not understand the significance of the procession, nor did he presume to inquire, but remained overcome by its sweetness. But when the whole procession had passed by, he summoned up courage and ran after those who walked last, and with great fear asked them: 'O dearest beings, I beg you of your kindness to tell me the meaning of these wonderful things, and of this noble procession.'

'Know, my son,' they replied, 'that we are all Friars Minor, who come from the glory of Paradise.'

And he asked: 'Who are these two, more resplendent than the others?'

They replied: 'They are Saint Francis and Saint Antony. And this last, whom you see so highly honoured, is a holy friar who died a short while ago. And because he fought so valiantly against temptation, and persevered to the end, we are escorting him in triumph to the glory of Paradise. And these fair silken robes which we wear were given us by God, in exchange for the rough habit that we wore patiently in Religion. And the glorious radiance which you see in us was given us by God in reward for the holy poverty, obedience, and chastity in which we served Him to the end. Therefore, son, think it no hardship to wear the sackcloth of Religion, which brings such a reward; for if, by wearing this sackcloth of Saint Francis for love of Christ, you despise the world, mortify the body, and fight bravely against the devil, you will receive a robe like ours and the same radiance of glory.'

At these words the young man came to himself, and confessed his fault before the Guardian and the friars; and thenceforward he took pleasure in the strictness of the penance and the roughness of the habit, and ended his life in the Order in great holiness.

CHAPTER 20: *How Saint Francis delivered the city of Gubbio from a fierce wolf*

AT a time when Saint Francis was living in the city of Gubbio, a huge wolf appeared in the neighbourhood. He was terrible and ferocious, and not only devoured beasts but human beings, so that all the townspeople lived in great fear, because he had often approached the city. Everyone went armed when they ventured out of the town, but despite all this no one was able to protect himself if he encountered the beast alone. And for fear of this wolf matters had come to such a pass that no one dared leave the city.

Saint Francis felt great compassion for the people of the place because of this, and wished to go out and meet the wolf; but all the townsfolk begged him not to do so. But he made the sign of the cross and went out into the country with his companions, putting his whole trust in God. And when the others were unwilling to go any further, Saint Francis made his way to the place where the wolf had his lair. Now when the wolf saw the crowd of townspeople who had come out to watch this miracle, he rushed at Saint Francis with open jaws. And as he approached, Saint Francis made the sign of the cross over him, and called to him, saying: 'Come here, Brother Wolf. In the name of Christ I command you not to attack me or anyone else.' And wonderful to tell, immediately Saint Francis made the sign of the cross, the terrible wolf closed his jaws and halted in his charge. And he obeyed Saint Francis's command, and came to lie down at his feet as gently as a lamb.

Then Saint Francis said to him: 'Brother Wolf, you have done great harm in these parts, and committed many grave crimes, ravaging and slaying God's creatures without His leave. Not only have you killed and eaten beasts, but have dared to kill and devour men, who are made in the likeness of God. For these things you deserve to hang as a robber and vile murderer: all the people cry out in complaint against you, and the whole district hates you. But I wish to make peace between you and them, and if you will commit no more crimes against them, they will forgive your past crimes, and neither men nor hounds will hunt you any more.'

At these words, by the movements of his body, tail, and eyes, and by bowing his head, the wolf showed that he accepted Saint Francis's proposal, and was willing to observe it. Then Saint Francis said: 'Brother Wolf, since you are ready to make this peace and keep it, I undertake that your food shall be regularly provided by the people of this district as long as you shall live, so that you will not suffer hunger any more; for I know well that you did all this evil because of hunger. But since I have obtained this favour for you, Brother Wolf, I want you to promise me that you will never again hurt man or beast. Do you promise this?' And by bowing his head, the wolf gave a clear sign that he promised. Then Saint Francis said: 'Brother Wolf, I want you to pledge me your good faith on this promise, for without this I cannot trust you.' And when Saint Francis held out his hand to receive the pledge, the wolf raised his paw and placed it gently in Saint Francis's hand, giving proof of his good faith as best he could.

Then Saint Francis said: 'Brother Wolf, in the name of Jesus Christ I command you to come with me. Trust me, and we will go and ratify this peace in the name of God.' And the wolf obediently went with him, as gentle as a lamb. When the townsfolk saw this, they were utterly dumbfounded, and the news immediately spread throughout the neighbourhood, so that all the people, great and small, men and women, young and old, hurried to the town square to see the wolf with Saint Francis.

And when all the people were gathered there, Saint Francis rose and preached to them, telling them among other things how that it was on account of sins that God allowed such calamities. 'The flames of hell, which the damned will have to endure for ever,' said Saint Francis, 'are far more terrible than the fangs of a wolf, that can do no more than destroy the body. How much more should men fear the jaws of hell, when so many people stand in fear and terror of so small a beast? Therefore return to God, dearest people, and do fitting penance for your sins, and God will deliver you from the

wolf in this present life and from the fires of hell in the life
to come.' And Saint Francis ended his sermon by saying:
'Listen, my brothers. Brother Wolf, who stands here before
you, has promised and given me his pledge to make peace
with you, and never to offend you in any way if you promise
to provide him with the food he needs each day. And I will
stand surety for him that he will faithfully observe this pact
of peace.'

Then with one accord the people promised to feed the
wolf every day. And Saint Francis said to the wolf before
them all: 'And you, Brother Wolf, do you promise to keep
the pact of peace with them, and never to hurt man, nor
beast, nor any other creature?' And the wolf knelt down and
bowed his head, and by gentle movements of his body, tail,
and ears showed as best he could that he was ready to keep
his pact with them. Then Saint Francis said: 'Brother Wolf,
outside the gates you gave me your pledge to keep this
promise: now I want you to give me this pledge in front of
all the people, that you will not betray me in the promise I
have made for you.' And raising his right paw, the wolf
placed it in Saint Francis's hand.

While these things were taking place, all the people were
filled with such admiration and joy, both out of their devotion to the Saint and because of the unique nature of the
miracle and the pact made with the wolf, that they all began
to shout to heaven, praising and blessing God who had sent
Saint Francis to them, and by his merits delivered them from
this cruel beast.

After this the wolf lived two years in Gubbio, and he used
to enter the houses in a friendly way, going from door to
door without harming anyone or anyone harming him. The
people fed him kindly, and as he went about the town, not
a single dog barked at him. At length, after two years, Brother
Wolf died of old age, and the townsfolk were deeply grieved,
for whenever they had seen him going so gently about the

town, they remembered more vividly the virtue and holiness of Saint Francis.*

CHAPTER 21: *How a lad gave Saint Francis some turtle-doves, which would not fly away until he had given them leave*

A LAD had once caught some turtle-doves, and was carrying them away to sell. He was met by Saint Francis, who always had an especial sympathy for gentle creatures, and looking at the doves with pitying eyes, he said to the lad: 'My good lad, I beg you give me these doves, for they are gentle and innocent birds, to which Holy Scripture compares pure, humble, and faithful souls. Don't allow them to fall into the hands of cruel men who would kill them.' Moved by God, the lad immediately gave them all to Saint Francis, who took them to his breast and began to speak soothingly to them, saying: 'O my little sisters, simple, innocent, pure doves, why have you let yourselves be caught? Now I wish to save you from death and make nests for you, so that you can be fruitful and multiply as God your Maker ordained.'

And Saint Francis went and made nests for all of them; and they used these nests, laid their eggs, and hatched them under the eyes of the friars. And they were so tame and friendly with Saint Francis and the friars that they might have been chickens reared by them. They would never fly away until Saint Francis had given them leave to go with his blessing. And Saint Francis told the lad: 'One day you will become a friar in this Order, and serve God.' And so it came about, for this lad became a friar, and lived in the Order in great holiness.

* To those who doubt the accuracy of this story, it is worth mentioning that its probability is supported by two independent facts: (i) It is recorded that the neighbourhood was threatened by packs of hungry wolves at the period of Francis's visit to Gubbio. (ii) The skull of a large wolf has been discovered beneath the walls of the old church of San Francesco della Pace. This was clearly placed there deliberately, and may well be that of the wolf in the story.

CHAPTER 22: *How Saint Francis saw the whole friary surrounded by devils, and how only one gained entry*

ONCE when Saint Francis was at prayer in the friary of the Porziuncula he saw by divine revelation the whole friary surrounded and besieged by devils, as though by a great army; but none of them were able to gain entry because the friars were so saintly that the devils could not enter through any of them. However, they persevered until one of the friars was angered by another, and pondered in his mind how he could accuse him and take revenge on him. And by this means, while this evil thought occupied his mind, a devil found the way open to him, and entering the friary, seated himself on this friar's neck.

The watchful shepherd, who was always on guard over his flock, saw that the wolf had entered to devour his lamb, and immediately called the friar to him. And he ordered him instantly to confess the poisonous hatred that he felt for his neighbour, through which he had fallen into the hands of the enemy. Horrified to learn that the holy father knew everything, he admitted all his venom and rancour, confessed his fault, and humbly begged for penance and mercy. This done, as soon as the friar had been absolved from his sin and received his penance, the devil fled from the presence of Saint Francis. And the friar, released from the clutches of the cruel creature by the kindness of his good shepherd, gave thanks to God, and returned corrected and amended to the holy shepherd's flock, in which he continued thenceforward in great sanctity.

CHAPTER 23: *How Saint Francis went to convert the Sultan of Babylon*

FIRED by zeal for the faith of Christ and by desire for martyrdom, Saint Francis once crossed the sea with twelve of his holiest companions in order to go directly to the Sultan of Babylon.* And they reached a country of the Saracens where the frontiers were guarded by men so cruel that no Christian who passed that way could escape being put to death. It pleased God, however, that they should not be killed, but they were captured, beaten, and bound, and taken before the Sultan.

As he stood before him, Saint Francis was inspired by the Holy Spirit, and preached with great devotion on the faith of Christ, for whose sake he was ready to pass through fire. As a result, the Sultan began to feel a great respect for him, both for the constancy of his faith and contempt for the world – for despite his utter poverty, he refused to accept any gift – and because of his evident desire for martyrdom. And thenceforward the Sultan listened to him readily, and asked him to return often; and he gladly gave him and his companions permission to preach wherever they pleased. He also gave them a pass-token, so that no one should molest them.

Having received this permission, Saint Francis sent his chosen companions two and two into various regions of the Saracens' country to preach the faith of Christ. He himself, with one companion, chose a road and travelled along it until he came to an inn to rest. Within it was a woman who was outwardly very beautiful but inwardly corrupt, and this wretched creature tempted him to sin. Saint Francis said: 'I am willing; let us go to bed.' And she led him to her room. Then Saint Francis said: 'Come with me', and he led her to a hot fire that was burning in the room, and in fervour of spirit he stripped himself naked and lay down before the fire on the hot hearth. And he invited her to come and strip and

* The Sultan Melek-el-Kamil, then engaged in war against the Crusading armies in Egypt under Duke Leopold of Austria during the winter of 1219. After this inconclusive visit to the Sultan, Saint Francis made a pilgrimage to the Holy Places.

lie down with him on this soft and beautiful bed. And when Saint Francis had remained there a long time with a cheerful face, and was neither burned nor scorched, the woman was frightened and pricked in conscience by such a miracle; and not only did she repent of her sinfulness and wicked intention, but was fully converted to the Faith of Christ. And she attained such holiness that many souls found salvation through her example in that country.

Finding at length that he could do no more good in those parts, Saint Francis was guided by God to recall his companions and return among the faithful. And when they had all assembled, he went back to the Sultan and took leave of him. Then the Sultan said: 'Francis, I would gladly accept the Faith of Christ, but I dare not do so at present, for if others heard of it, they would murder both me, you, and all your companions. And because I know that you can still do much good, and because I have to decide many affairs of great importance, I have no wish to bring about your death or my own. But instruct me how I can be saved, and I am willing to do whatever you tell me.'

Then Saint Francis said: 'My Lord, I must now take leave of you; but when I have returned to my own land, and by God's grace have reached heaven after my death, I will – God willing – send two of my friars to you. From them you shall receive Christian Baptism and be saved, as my Lord Jesus Christ has revealed to me. Meanwhile shun everything that hinders the grace of God, so that, when it comes to you, it may find you rightly disposed to faith and devotion.' And the Sultan did as he had promised.

After this Saint Francis left with the venerable company of his holy companions, and after some years he died and yielded up his soul to God. The Sultan also fell sick, and expecting the fulfilment of Saint Francis's promise, he had guards stationed at certain passes. And he gave orders that if two friars in the habit of Saint Francis should appear, they

were to be brought to him without delay. At that time Saint
Francis appeared to two friars, and told them to hasten to the
Sultan immediately, and effect the salvation of his soul as
he had promised. So these friars set out at once, crossed the
sea, and were escorted by guards to the Sultan.

When the Sultan saw them, he was filled with joy, and said:
'Now I know for certain that God has sent His servants for
my salvation, in fulfilment of the promise that Saint Francis
made me by divine revelation.' And when he had received
instruction from the friars, and had been born again in Christ
by Baptism, he died of his illness, and his soul was saved
through the prayers of Saint Francis.

CHAPTER 24: *How Saint Francis healed a leper in body and soul*

SAINT FRANCIS, the true disciple of Christ, while still in
this life of misery, strove with all his might to follow Christ,
the perfect Master. So it often came about that those who
were healed in body were at the same time healed in soul by
the power of God, as we read of Christ Himself. And for this
reason Saint Francis gladly served the lepers himself, and
ordered that the friars of his Order, wherever they lived
throughout the world, should serve the lepers for the love
of Christ, who for our sakes was willing to be treated like a
leper.

At a place near where Saint Francis was living, it once happened that the friars were serving in a hospital for lepers and
other sick folk. Among these was a leper so bad-tempered,
unbearable, and stubborn that everyone believed him possessed by the devil, as indeed he was. Not only did he abuse and
strike everyone who served him in a most shameful way, but,
what was worse, uttered foul blasphemies against Christ and
His most holy Mother, so that no one could be found willing
or able to serve him. And although the friars tried to bear

the insults and abuse directed against themselves, so as to increase the merit of patience, they could not in conscience endure his insults against Christ and His Mother, so decided to leave him alone altogether. But they did not wish to do this until they had duly reported the matter to Saint Francis.

When Saint Francis had listened to their account, he went to this perverse leper himself, and as he approached, he greeted him saying, 'God give you peace, my dearest brother.' The leper answered roughly: 'What peace can I have from God, who has deprived me of peace and every good thing, and made me utterly rotten and stinking?'

And Saint Francis said: 'My son, be patient. The infirmities of the body are given us by God in this world in order to save our souls; for they bring great merit when we bear them patiently.'

The sick man replied: 'And how can I endure the pain that torments me day and night with patience? Not only am I plagued by my disease, but even worse by the friars whom you ordered to serve me, and who do not look after me as they ought?'

Then Saint Francis, knowing by divine revelation that the leper was possessed by an evil spirit, went away and entered into prayer. And he prayed God very earnestly for the man, and afterwards he returned to him and said:

'My son, since you are not satisfied with the others, I would like to look after you myself.'

'That suits me,' said the man. 'But what can you do for me that the others cannot do?'

'I will do whatever you wish,' Saint Francis replied. The sick man replied: 'I'd like you to wash me all over, because I stink so horribly that I cannot endure myself.'

Then Saint Francis at once ordered water to be heated, and many fragrant herbs to be placed in it; after that he stripped the man and began to wash him with his own hands, while another friar poured the water. And by a divine miracle, wherever Saint Francis touched him with his holy hands, the leprosy vanished, and the flesh became perfectly healthy. And as his flesh began to heal, so did his soul begin to heal. When the leper realized that his leprosy was being cleansed, he began to feel deep compunction and repentance for his sins, and to weep most bitterly; so that while his body was outwardly cleansed by its bathing in water, his soul within him was cleansed from sin by contrition and tears. And when he was perfectly healed both in body and soul, he humbly confessed his guilt, and exclaimed weeping: 'Alas! I deserve hell for the insults and injuries that I have inflicted on the friars, and for my impatience and blasphemy against God.' Then for fifteen days he continued weeping bitterly for his sins and imploring God's mercy, and made full confession to a priest. And when Saint Francis saw the unmistakable miracle which God had wrought through his hands, he gave thanks to God and left the place, and he went away to a distant part, for his humility moved him to avoid all wordly glory, and in everything that he did he sought only the honour and glory of God, and not his own.

It later pleased God that this leper, healed in body and soul, fell sick of another complaint, and after fifteen days of penance, fortified by the sacraments of the Church, he died a holy death and his soul entered Paradise. In evidence of this he appeared in the air to Saint Francis while he was at prayer, and said: 'Do you remember me?'

'Who are you?' asked Saint Francis.

'I am the leper whom Christ the Blessed healed through your merits,' he replied. 'I am now about to enter eternal life. For this I thank God and you. May you be blessed in soul and body; and blessed be your words and deeds, for many souls in this world will be saved through you. And be sure of this, that not a day will pass in which the holy angels and all the saints will not thank God for the holy work accomplished by you and your Order in different parts of the world.

So be comforted, and thank God, and may His blessing rest on you.' And with these words he went to heaven, and Saint Francis remained greatly comforted.

CHAPTER 25: *How Saint Francis received into the Order a young man who drove away some robbers, and how Saint Francis sent him after them with food, and in so doing converted them*

ONE day Saint Francis was travelling through the Borgo district to San Sepolcro, and as he passed a castle called Monte Casale, there came to him a young nobleman, brought up in luxury, who said: 'Father, I have a great desire to become one of your friars.'

Saint Francis replied: 'Son, you are a young man who has been reared in luxury; it is likely that you could not endure our poverty and hardship.'

But he said: 'Father, are you not men like myself? If you can endure them, so can I, if God gives me grace.'

Saint Francis was pleased with this reply, so he gave him his blessing and received him into the Order at once, giving him the name of Brother Angelo. And the young man showed such signs of grace that after a short while Saint Francis appointed him Guardian of the friary at Monte Casale.

At that time the district was troubled by three notorious robbers, who had committed many crimes in the countryside. One day these ruffians came to the friary and asked Brother Angelo the Guardian to give them food. The Guardian rebuked them severely, answering: 'Robbers and cruel murderers! You feel no shame in robbing others of what they earn; in addition you are so conceited and impudent that you want to devour the offerings given to the servants of God. You aren't fit to cumber the earth, for you have no respect for man and none for God who made you. So be off with you, and don't appear here again!' And disconcerted by his rebuke, they went away very indignant.

Afterwards Saint Francis came in with a satchel of bread and a flask of wine which he and his companions had begged. And when the Guardian told him how he had driven away the robbers, Saint Francis sharply rebuked him, telling him that he had behaved cruelly. 'Sinners are brought back to God by kindness better than by harsh rebukes,' he said. 'That is why our Lord and Master, whose Gospel way we have vowed to follow, says that it is not the healthy but the sick who need the doctor, and that He had not come to call the just, but sinners to repentance; and that is why He often ate with them. By acting in this manner you have acted contrary to charity, and contrary to the Gospel of Christ, so I order you under holy obedience to take this satchel of bread that I have begged, and this flask of wine, and search for them immediately over the hill and dale until you find them. Offer them this bread and wine from me: then kneel down before them and humbly confess your sin of cruelty. And beg them from me not to act wickedly any more, but to fear God and offend their neighbour no more. And if they will do this, I promise to supply their needs, and always provide them with food and drink. And when you have done this, humbly return here.'

While the Guardian went to carry out this order, Saint Francis himself entered into prayer, and asked God to soften the hearts of these robbers and bring them to repentance. And when he had overtaken them, the obedient Guardian offered them the bread and wine, and did as Saint Francis had told him. And it pleased God that while the robbers were consuming Saint Francis's gift, they began to say to one another: 'Alas for us, miserable wretches! What awful punishments await us in hell! For we go around robbing, beating, and wounding our neighbours, and even murdering them. And despite the many wicked and disgraceful things that we have done, we feel no remorse of conscience nor fear of God. Look at this holy friar who has come to us; for a few words justly spoken about our wickedness, he has humbly confessed his fault. More than this, he has brought bread and wine, and a most generous promise from the holy father. These friars are certainly saints of God, who deserve Paradise; but we are sons of everlasting damnation, and deserve the pains of hell, daily adding to our own punishment. And after all the sins we have committed until now, we do not know whether we can find mercy with God.'

Such were the sentiments expressed by one of them, and the other two said: 'What you say is certainly true; but what should we do?'

'Let us go to Saint Francis,' said the first, 'and if he holds out any hope that we can find mercy with God for our sins, let us do whatever he orders, and we may be able to save our souls from the pains of hell.'

This advice pleased the others, so by mutual consent they went to Saint Francis and said: 'Father, we do not think that we can find mercy with God, because of many horrible sins we have committed. But if you have any hope that God will receive us with mercy, we are ready to do whatever you say, and do penance with you.'

Then Saint Francis, receiving them very charitably and kindly, comforted them with many examples, and assured them of God's mercy. And he promised them that they would certainly obtain it from God, whose mercy is infinite; and he told them that, even if our sins were without number, yet the mercy of God is greater, as we are told in the Gospel and by the Apostle Saint Paul: 'Christ the Blessed came into this world to save sinners.'

Instructed by these words and similar sayings, the three robbers renounced the devil and all his works. And Saint Francis admitted them into the Order, and they began to perform strict penance. Two of them lived only a short while after their conversion, and went to Paradise. But the third lived on, and in atonement for his sins set himself to perform such penances that for fifteen consecutive years – except for Lent, which he observed with the other friars – he always fasted three days a week on bread and water, went barefoot, possessed only one habit, and never slept after Matins.

About this time Saint Francis passed from this life of sorrows, and this friar had by now continued these penances for many years. One night after Matins there came upon him such an overwhelming temptation to sleep that he could not resist it, or keep his usual vigil. At length, unable either to resist sleep or to pray, he retired to his bed to sleep, and as soon as he laid down his head, he entered into rapture, and was carried away in spirit to a very high mountain. A sheer precipice fell away from it, and on both sides projected shattered, jagged crags and sharp ledges, so that it was an awe-inspiring scene to look upon. And an angel who was leading this friar gave him a push and thrust him over the precipice, so that he hurtled down and rebounded from rock to rock and boulder to boulder, until at last he found himself at the bottom of the precipice; and it seemed to him that he was utterly broken and shattered. And as he lay on the ground in this sorry state, his angel-guide said to him: 'Get up, for you have still a long way to go.'

The friar answered: 'You must be stupid and cruel; you see me nearly dying from the fall that you caused, and yet you tell me to get up.' Then the angel came to him, and at his touch all his limbs were healed and restored.

Then the angel showed him a wide plain covered with sharp, cutting stones and with thorns and briars, and he told him to cross the whole of this plain barefoot until he arrived at the end. And when the friar had crossed the whole plain with great difficulty and pain, the angel said to him: 'Enter that furnace, for you must needs do so.'

The friar replied: 'Alas, what a cruel guide you are to me!

You see me near to death after crossing this agonizing plain, and now instead of letting me rest you order me to enter that blazing furnace.' And as he looked about him, he saw many devils standing round the furnace with forks in their hands, and when he was slow to enter, they quickly thrust him in with them. Once inside the furnace, he saw a man who had been a relation of his enveloped in flames, and asked him: 'Unhappy kinsman, how did you come here?' And he replied: 'Go on a little further, and you will find my wife, your cousin, who will tell you the cause of our damnation.' So the friar went a little further, and saw his kinswoman all aflame, enclosed in a burning grain-measure. And he asked her: 'Unhappy and wretched cousin, how did you come into this horrible torment?'

She replied: 'Because at the time of the great famine that Saint Francis predicted, my husband and I falsified the measures of grain and wheat which we sold; and that is why I am burning, shut up in this measure.'

After this the angel-guide pushed the friar out of the furnace, and said: 'Prepare yourself for a terrible journey that you must now undertake.'

And he complained, saying: 'O most relentless of guides, you have no pity on me. You can see that I am all scorched by that furnace, and now you want to take me on a dangerous and horrible journey.' Then the angel touched him, and made him whole and strong. And he led him to a bridge which could not be crossed without great danger, for it was very frail and narrow, and extremely slippery, without any hand-rail. And beneath it flowed a terrible river, full of serpents, dragons, and scorpions, which emitted a foul stench.

And the angel said: 'Cross this bridge, for you must needs do so.'

And the friar replied: 'How can I cross it without falling into this dangerous river?'

The angel said: 'Follow me, and set your foot where you

see me set mine, and you will cross in safety.' So the friar crossed behind the angel until they reached the middle of the bridge; and having gone so far, the angel flew away and left him, alighting on a very lofty mountain far beyond the bridge. The friar gazed long at the place to which the angel had flown, but abandoned without a guide and looking downward, he saw the horrifying beasts waiting with their heads out of the water and their jaws agape, ready to devour him if he fell. And he was so terrified that he had no notion what to do or say, for he could neither turn back nor go forward.

Then, realizing the gravity of his plight, and knowing that he had no refuge save in God alone, he knelt down, and holding firmly to the bridge commended himself to God with his whole heart and many tears, imploring Him in His most holy mercy to aid him. As he ended his prayer, it seemed to him that he began to grow wings, so he waited with great joy until they should grow and enable him to fly up from the bridge to the place whither the angel had flown. After an interval, incited by his strong desire to cross the bridge, he attempted to fly; but, because his wings were not strong enough, he fell back on to the bridge and the feathers dropped out. So he clung to the bridge again, and commended himself to God as before.

When he had prayed, he seemed to grow wings again, but, as before, he did not wait until they were fully grown; so, trying to fly before the time, he fell back on to the bridge once more, and the feathers dropped out. Realizing at length that it was his haste to fly before the time that caused him to fall, he began to say to himself: 'If I grow wings the third time, I shall wait until they are strong enough to enable me to fly without falling.' And as he continued in these thoughts, he found himself growing wings for the third time, and he waited a long time until they were well grown. And it seemed to him that between the first and second growth of his wings he had waited at least a hundred and fifty years.

At length he rose for the third time, and, exerting all his strength, took flight and reached the high place where the angel had alighted. And he knocked at the gate of the palace to which the angel had flown, and the porter asked him: 'Who are you to come here?'

He answered: 'I am a Friar Minor.'

'Wait,' said the porter, 'for I wish to fetch Saint Francis to see whether he knows you.' While he went to find Saint Francis, the friar began to gaze around at the wonderful walls of this palace, which appeared to be translucent with so bright a light that he could clearly see the choirs of saints, and all that was happening inside.

And as he was gazing in wonder, Saint Francis appeared with Brother Bernard and Brother Giles; and behind Saint Francis came so great a company of holy men and women who had followed his way of life that they seemed almost innumerable. When Saint Francis arrived, he said to the porter: 'Allow him to enter, for he is one of my friars.' And as soon as he had entered, he experienced such sweetness that he forgot all the tribulations he had undergone as though they had never occurred. Then Saint Francis led him inside and showed him many marvellous things, and he said to him: 'My son, you must return to the world and remain there seven days. During this time prepare yourself carefully and devoutly, for after seven days I will come for you, and you shall dwell with me in this home of the blessed.'

Saint Francis was clothed in a marvellous mantle, adorned with the loveliest stars, and his five Stigmata were like five stars, shining with such splendour that the whole palace was illumined by their rays. And Brother Bernard wore on his head a glorious diadem of stars, and Brother Giles was enveloped in a marvellous light. And with them he recognized many other saints whom he had never seen in this world. Then having taken leave of Saint Francis, he returned most unwillingly to the world, and awoke. And as he came to himself and regained consciousness, the friars were ringing the bell for Prime, so that the vision had lasted only from Matins to Prime, although it had seemed to him that it had lasted many years. Seven days after he had related the whole vision he fell sick of a fever, and on the eighth day Saint Francis came for him as he had promised with a great company of glorious saints, and led his soul to the kingdom of the blessed and to everlasting life.

CHAPTER 26: *How Saint Francis went to Bologna, and converted two distinguished scholars by his preaching*

ONCE, when Saint Francis visited the city of Bologna, all the people rushed out to meet him, and the crowds were so dense that he had great difficulty in reaching the square, which was filled with men, women, and scholars. Saint Francis mounted a high place in the middle of the square and began to preach as the Holy Spirit moved him; and he preached so wonderfully that his words seemed those of an angel rather than of a man. They were so divinely inspired that they seemed like sharp arrows, piercing the hearts of all who heard him, so that a great number of men and women were converted to penitence during his preaching.

Among these were two scholars of noble birth from the March of Ancona; one was named Pellegrino and the other Riccieri, both of whom were touched to the heart by divine inspiration as a result of his sermon. And they came to Saint Francis, declaring that they were firmly resolved to renounce the world and become friars. Then Saint Francis, knowing by divine revelation that they had been sent by God and would lead a holy life in the Order, and recognizing their deep fervour, welcomed them gladly, and said to them: 'You, Pellegrino, will lead the life of humility, and you, Riccieri, will serve the brethren.' And so it came about, for Brother

Pellegrino did not wish to become a priest, but to remain a layman, although he was very learned and well acquainted with canon law. And through his humility he attained great perfection of virtue, insomuch that Brother Bernard, the 'first-born' of Saint Francis, said that he was one of the most perfect friars in the world. In due course Brother Pellegrino passed from this life to the life of heaven, performing many miracles both before and after his death.

Brother Riccieri served the brethren devoutly and faithfully, living in great holiness and humility, and became very intimate with Saint Francis, who revealed many secrets to him. He became Minister of the Province of the March of Ancona, and ruled it for a long time in the greatest peace and wisdom. After a while, however, God allowed a very severe temptation to beset his soul, and this caused him great trouble and distress, so that he disciplined himself by fasting, scourging, and tears, day and night. But he could not banish this temptation, and was often in despair because he thought himself abandoned by God. During one of these times of despair he decided as a last remedy to go to Saint Francis, thinking to himself: 'If Saint Francis receives me kindly and shows his customary friendship towards me, I will believe that God may yet have pity on me; but if not, it will be a sign that I am abandoned by God.'

So Brother Riccieri went to visit Saint Francis, who at the time was lying gravely ill in the palace of the Bishop of Assisi. And God revealed to Saint Francis the whole nature of that friar's temptation and despair, and he was aware of his purpose and coming. And Saint Francis at once called Brother Leo and Brother Masseo, and said to them: 'Go and meet my very dear son Brother Riccieri: embrace him for me, and welcome him, and tell him that of all the friars in the world I have an especial love for him.' So they went out and found Brother Riccieri on the road, and they embraced him and gave him the message as Saint Francis had directed them. And immediately his soul was filled with such comfort and sweetness that he was almost beside himself. And thanking God with all his heart, he went on and came to the place where Saint Francis was lying sick.

Although Saint Francis was gravely ill, when he heard Brother Riccieri approaching, he got up and came to meet him. And embracing him affectionately, he said: 'Brother Riccieri, dearest son, out of all the friars in the world I have an especial love for you.' And so saying, he made the sign of the holy cross on his forehead and kissed him there. Then he continued: 'Dearest son, God has allowed you to suffer that temptation for your own great merit and gain; but if you no longer desire that gain, you need not have it.' Wonderful to tell, directly Saint Francis had uttered these words, all temptation suddenly left him, as though he had never felt it in his life, and he remained completely at peace.

CHAPTER 27: *How Brother Bernard da Quintaville remained in ecstasy from Matins until None, as he contemplated the Body of Christ*

THE great grace which God often granted to the poor followers of the Gospel, who had forsaken the world for love of Christ, was especially evident in Brother Bernard da Quintaville, who, after he had taken the habit of Saint Francis, was many times rapt in God by contemplation of heavenly things. Among other occasions it once happened that while he was in church to hear Mass with his mind wholly uplifted to God, he became so absorbed and enraptured in contemplation that at the elevation of the Body of Christ he saw nothing, nor did he kneel or draw back his cowl as did the other friars present. But without moving his eyes, he remained with a fixed gaze, unconscious of everything from Matins until None. And returning to himself after None, he walked through the friary crying out in a voice full of wonder: 'O Brothers! O Brothers! O Brothers! There is no man in this country, however great or noble, who, if he were promised the most beautiful palace filled with gold, would not gladly carry a sackful of dung in order to gain so rich a treasure!'

The mind of this Brother Bernard was so constantly uplifted to God, and to this heavenly treasure promised to those that love Him, that for fifteen years he went about with his mind and face constantly raised to heaven. And during this time he never satisfied his hunger, although he ate a portion of whatever was placed before him; for he said that it is not perfect abstinence when a man does not enjoy his food, since perfect abstinence consists in self-denial in whatever things are pleasing to the taste. And through this abstinence he gained such clarity and enlightenment of mind that even learned clergy used to come to him to solve difficult and important questions, and to elucidate obscure passages of Scripture, and he cleared up every difficulty. And because his mind was entirely free from worldly matters, he was able to soar to the heights in contemplation like a swallow, so that he sometimes remained alone for twenty or thirty days on the summit of the highest mountains, rapt in contemplation of heavenly things. Because of this Brother Giles said of him that no other man had received such a gift as had been bestowed on Brother Bernard, namely, that he should feed as he flew, like the swallow. And because of this sublime favour he had received from God, Saint Francis used to converse with him freely and frequently both by day and night, so that sometimes they were both found rapt in God all night long in the wood where they had met to speak of God, who is blessed for evermore.

CHAPTER 28: *How, in order to deceive him, the devil appeared to Brother Ruffino in the form of Christ, and told him that he was damned*

BROTHER RUFFINO, one of the noblest men of Assisi, a companion of Saint Francis and a man of great holiness, was at one time violently beset and tempted by the devil on the matter of predestination. As a result he became very depressed and sad, because the devil put it into his head that he was damned and not among those predestined to eternal life, and that whatever he did in the Order would be wasted. Although this temptation persisted day after day, he was ashamed to disclose it to Saint Francis, although he did not abandon his prayers or the prescribed fasts. And because of this his enemy began to heap sorrow upon sorrow, and in addition to his inward conflict, he attacked him externally with false visions. On one occasion the devil appeared to him in the form of the Crucified, and said: 'O Brother Ruffino, why do you trouble yourself with penance and prayer, for you are not among those predestined to eternal life? Believe me, I know whom I have chosen and predestined. So pay no attention to the son of Pietro Bernadone if he tells you the contrary. Do not question him on this matter, for neither he nor anyone else knows it if not I, who am the Son of God. So take it as certain that you are among the number of the damned; nor has it pleased me to include the son of Pietro Bernadone your Father among the elect, neither you nor he. His own father is also damned, and whosoever follows him is deceived.'

With these words he suddenly vanished, and Brother Ruffino was plunged into such gloom by the Prince of Darkness that he lost all the trust and love he had for Saint Francis, and did not care to divulge anything.

But everything that Brother Ruffino did not tell the holy Father was revealed to him by the Holy Spirit, so when Saint

92

Francis saw in spirit how great a peril threatened this friar, he sent Brother Masseo to him. Brother Ruffino, however, answered roughly: 'What have I to do with Brother Francis?' Then Brother Masseo, filled with divine wisdom and recognizing the deception of the devil, said: 'O Brother Ruffino, don't you know that Brother Francis is like an angel of God, who has brought light to many souls in this world, and it is through him that we have received the grace of God? So I wish you to come and see him at once, for it is clear to me that you are deceived by the devil.'

At these words, Brother Ruffino rose and went to Saint Francis. And seeing him coming a long way off, Saint Francis called to him: 'O unhappy Brother Ruffino! To whom have you been listening?' And when Brother Ruffino came up to him, Saint Francis told him in detail all the temptations that he had had from the devil, both inward and outward, and he proved clearly to him that it was the devil who had appeared to him and not Christ, and that he should on no account listen to his suggestions. 'But when the devil says to you again, "You are damned", answer him, "Open your mouth, and I will drop my dung in it." And this shall be your proof that he is the devil, for directly you have given this reply, he will depart. By this same means you will realize that it was the devil, for he has hardened your heart against all good, which is his natural purpose; but Christ the Blessed never hardens the heart of the faithful, but melts it, as He has said through the mouth of the Prophet: "*I will take away their heart of stone, and give them a heart of flesh.*" ' *

Then Brother Ruffino, seeing how accurately Saint Francis described the whole course of his temptations, was touched by his words, and began to weep copiously and ask Saint Francis to pray for him; and he humbly confessed his fault in having concealed his temptation. So he remained fully reassured and comforted by the counsels of the holy father,

* Ezekiel xi, 19

and completely changed for the better. Then in conclusion Saint Francis said to him: 'Go and make your confession, and do not abandon your usual diligence in prayer. And rest assured that this temptation will be of great help and comfort to you: in a short while you will prove it.'

So Brother Ruffino went back to his cell in the wood, and continued in prayer with many tears. And the enemy appeared in the outward form of Christ, and said: 'Brother Ruffino, have I not told you that you shouldn't believe the son of Pietro Bernadone, and that there is no need for you to weary yourself with tears and prayers, seeing that you are damned? What is the good of troubling yourself in this life when you will be damned when you die?' And immediately Brother Ruffino replied: 'Open your mouth, and I will drop my dung in it.' At which the devil hurriedly departed in disgust, causing such a storm and commotion among the rocks on the high mountain near by that they were shattered, and the debris of fallen stones remained there for a long while. And as they rolled, the rocks struck against one another with such violence that they sparkled with an uncanny fire throughout the valley. And at the terrible rumbling that they caused Saint Francis and his companions came out of the friary astonished, to see what extraordinary thing had happened. One can still see this vast ruin of stones today.

Then Brother Ruffino knew clearly that it was the devil who had deceived him, and turning to Saint Francis, he threw himself to the ground in remorse, admitting his fault. And Saint Francis comforted him with tender words, and sent him wholly at peace to his cell, where he remained in devout prayer. And Christ the Blessed appeared to him, and kindled his whole soul with divine love, saying: 'My son, you have done well to trust Saint Francis, for it was the devil who distressed you. But I am Christ your Master, and in order to reassure you, I give you this sign: you shall feel no more sadness or gloom as long as you live.' With these words Christ departed, leaving him in such joy and sweetness of soul and such exaltation of mind that he remained in ecstasy throughout that day and night.

Thenceforward Brother Ruffino was so confirmed in grace and assured of his salvation that he was an entirely changed man, and, if the others had allowed him, he would have continued day and night in prayer and contemplation of divine things. Because of this Saint Francis used to say of him that Brother Ruffino had been canonized in this life by Jesus Christ, and except in his presence he did not hesitate to call him Saint Ruffino, although he was still living in this world.

CHAPTER 29: *How Saint Francis sent Brother Ruffino to preach naked in Assisi, and later, in order to make proof of his own mortification, went himself in the same state, gaining much spiritual benefit*

BY constant contemplation this same Brother Ruffino had become so absorbed in God that he was detached and silent, and very seldom spoke; moreover, he lacked the grace of preaching and possessed no eloquence. Despite this, Saint Francis ordered him to go into Assisi and preach to the people as God should move him. So Brother Ruffino answered: 'Reverend Father, I beg you to excuse me and not to send me; for as you know, I have not the grace of preaching, and I am simple and stupid.'

Then Saint Francis said: 'Because you have not obeyed me at once, I order you under holy obedience to go to Assisi stripped and wearing nothing but your under-garment. Then you are to enter a church and preach thus stripped to the people.'

At this command Brother Ruffino stripped himself, and went thus to Assisi, and entered a church. And when he had made a reverence to the altar, he mounted the pulpit and began to preach. At this the children and people began to laugh and said: 'See! These men practise such penances that they are robbed of their wits and beside themselves!'

Meanwhile Saint Francis, considering Brother Ruffino's prompt obedience, and how he had been one of the first gentlemen of Assisi, regretted the humiliating order he had given him, and began to reproach himself. And he said: 'Why have you acquired such presumption, son of Pietro Bernadone, miserable little creature, that you should order Brother Ruffino, one of the first gentlemen of Assisi, to go and preach to the people stripped like a lunatic? By God! You shall sample what you have ordered to others!' And in fervour of spirit, he immediately stripped himself naked in the same way and went into Assisi, taking Brother Leo with him to carry his habit and that of Brother Ruffino. And when the people of Assisi saw him in the same condition, they jeered at him, thinking that both he and Brother Ruffino had been driven mad by excessive penance.

As Saint Francis entered the church, Brother Ruffino was preaching in these words: 'O dearest friends, flee from the world, forsake sin, and make just return to others if you wish to escape hell. Keep the commandments of God by loving God and your neighbour if you wish to enter heaven; and do penance if you wish to possess the kingdom of heaven.'

Then Saint Francis, stripped as he was, mounted the pulpit and began to preach so wonderfully on contempt of the world, on holy penance, on voluntary poverty, on desire for the kingdom of heaven, and on the nakedness and humiliation of the Passion of our Lord Jesus Christ that everyone present at his preaching began to weep bitterly with deep devotion and heartfelt contrition. And both within the church and throughout Assisi there was such grief for the Passion of Christ that nothing like it had ever happened before.

And when the people had been edified and comforted by

the action of Saint Francis and Brother Ruffino, Saint Francis
helped Brother Ruffino to dress, and he put on his own habit.
And thus re-clothed they returned to the friary of the
Porziuncula, praising and glorifying God, who had given
them grace to overcome themselves by contempt of self, to
edify Christ's sheep by a good example, and to show them
the good results of despising the world. And on that day the
people's devotion to them increased so greatly that whosoever could touch the hem of their habits counted himself
blessed.

CHAPTER 30: *How by divine revelation Saint Francis knew
all the virtues and faults of his friars, and how he knew that
Brother Ruffino was canonized by Christ*

OUR LORD JESUS CHRIST says in the Gospel: 'I know My
sheep, and they know Me.' In the same way the blessed
Father Saint Francis, as a good shepherd, knew by divine revelation all the merits and virtues of his companions, and recognized their failings. And, as can be seen in the revelations that
he received about his earliest followers, he always knew how
to apply the best remedy, that is, by humbling the proud,
exalting the humble, rebuking vice, and praising virtue.

Among such instances we hear that Saint Francis was once
in a certain friary talking to his companions about God. And
Brother Ruffino was not with them, but was in the wood
engaged in contemplation; during the discussion, however,
Brother Ruffino came out of the wood, and passed at some
distance from them. When Saint Francis saw him, he turned
to his companions and asked: 'Tell me, whose do you think
is the holiest soul that God possesses in the world?' And they
answered that it was his own.

'Dearest brothers, I am the most worthless man that God
has in this world,' said Saint Francis. 'But you see Brother

Ruffino, who has just come out of the wood? God has revealed to me that his soul is one of the three most holy souls that He possesses in the world. And I declare that I would not hesitate to call him Saint Ruffino during his lifetime, for his soul is established in grace, hallowed in heaven, and canonized by our Lord Jesus Christ.' But Saint Francis never used these words in the presence of Brother Ruffino.

In the same way Saint Francis recognized the faults of his friars. He clearly understood Brother Elias, whom he often took to task for his pride; he also predicted that Brother John della Cappella would hang himself by the neck. So, too, in the case of the friar whom the devil grasped by the throat when he was corrected for disobedience, and many other friars whose faults and virtues he knew clearly through the revelation of God.

CHAPTER 31: *How Brother Masseo desired the virtue of humility, and was willing to give his eyes to possess it; and how at length he obtained it*

THE first companions of Saint Francis strove with all their might to be poor in worldly goods and rich in virtue, through which a man may win the true and eternal riches of heaven. It came about one day that they were assembled to talk about God, and one of them gave this illustration: 'There was once a man who was a great friend of God, and possessed great grace both in the active and contemplative life. With it he had also such great and profound humility that he regarded himself as the greatest of sinners, and this humility sanctified and established him in grace, enabling him constantly to grow in virtue and the gifts of God, and never allowing him to fall into sin.'

As Brother Masseo listened to the wonderful qualities of humility and recognized that it contained the treasures of eternal life, he began to be so fired with love and desire for this virtue of humility that, raising his face to heaven in great fervour, he made a vow and firm resolve never again to take pleasure in this world until he should feel this virtue perfectly established within his soul. Thenceforward he remained almost confined to his cell, mortifying himself by fasting, prayer, and heartfelt tears before God in order to win this virtue, without which he considered himself deserving of hell, and with which that friend of God of whom he had heard had been so richly endowed.

When Brother Masseo had remained constant in this desire for many days, one day he happened to enter the wood, and he walked through it in fervour of spirit giving vent to tears, sighs, and exclamations, imploring God with fervent longing to grant him this divine virtue. And because God is pleased to grant the prayers of the humble and contrite, as Brother Masseo was thus engaged, there came a voice from heaven, calling him twice: 'Brother Masseo! Brother Masseo!' And, knowing in spirit that it was the voice of Christ, he answered, 'My Lord! My Lord!'

And Christ said to him: 'What will you give to possess the grace that you ask?'

Brother Masseo replied: 'My Lord, I am ready to give the eyes out of my head.'

And Christ said to him: 'And I will that you possess this grace and keep your eyes.' And with these words the voice ceased.

And Brother Masseo remained filled with such grace of the desired virtue of humility and with the light of God that thenceforward he was constantly in a state of jubilation, and as he prayed he used often to make a glad sound like the deep cooing of doves. And he would remain thus in contemplation with a radiant face and joyful heart, and as he had now become perfectly humble, he regarded himself as the least of all men in the world. And on being asked by Brother

James of Fallerone why in his gladness he never changed his note, he replied with deep joy that when one found complete satisfaction in a single note there was no need to alter it.

CHAPTER 32: *How, in obedience to the Pope, Saint Clare blessed the food at table, and how by a miracle the cross appeared imprinted on every loaf*

SAINT CLARE, the most devout disciple of the Cross of Christ and noble plant of our master Saint Francis, was of such holiness that not only the Bishops and Cardinals, but even the Pope himself had a great desire to see and hear her, and he often came to visit her in person. On one occasion when he* visited the convent to hear her speak of heavenly and divine things, and while they were discussing spiritual matters, Saint Clare ordered the tables to be laid and bread placed on them for the Holy Father to bless. So when their spiritual converse was ended, Saint Clare knelt with great reverence and asked him to be pleased to bless the loaves set on the table.

The Holy Father replied: 'My very faithful Sister Clare, it is Our wish that you bless this bread, and make over it the sign of Christ's Cross, to which you have so completely devoted yourself.'

And Saint Clare said: 'Most Holy Father, I beg you to excuse me, for I would deserve the severest rebuke were I, a worthless woman, to presume to give such a blessing in the presence of the Vicar of Christ.'

And the Pope answered: 'So that this cannot be regarded as presumption, but as a meritorious act of obedience, We order you under holy obedience to make the sign of the Cross over these loaves and to bless them in the name of God.'

Then Saint Clare, as a true daughter of obedience, very

* Pope Gregory IX.

devoutly blessed the loaves with the sign of the Cross. And, marvellous to tell, the sign of the Cross immediately appeared imprinted on each of them. Then a portion of this bread was eaten, and a portion set aside because of the miracle. And when the Holy Father had seen this miracle, he took some of the bread, and giving thanks to God, departed, leaving Saint Clare with his blessing.

At that time there lived in the convent Sister Ortolana, mother of Saint Clare, and Sister Agnes, her own sister; both of them, like Saint Clare, were filled with virtue and the Holy Spirit, and with them were many other holy nuns. And Saint Francis used to send many sick people to them, and they restored them to health by their prayers and by the sign of the Cross.

CHAPTER 33: *How Saint Louis came to visit Brother Giles, whom he had never seen, and how they understood one another without speaking*

SAINT LOUIS, King of France, went on pilgrimage to the holy places throughout the world, and hearing the highest reports of the holiness of Brother Giles, who had been one of Saint Francis's first companions, he set his heart on visiting him in person. For this purpose he came to Perugia, where Brother Giles was then living, and coming to the door of the friary as a poor unknown pilgrim with a few companions, he asked with great insistence for Brother Giles, saying nothing about who it was that asked for him.

The porter went and told Brother Giles that a pilgrim stood at the door asking for him, and God revealed to him in spirit that it was the King of France. Full of fervour he immediately left his cell and ran to the door, and, although they had never seen one another, they both knelt down most devoutly without further questioning, and embraced and kissed one another with such familiarity that they might have been the closest of friends for a long time. But during the whole meeting neither spoke to the other, but remained in a silent embrace, the outward sign of their loving charity. And after they had remained thus for a long while without uttering a word, they took leave of one another, Saint Louis continuing on his journey and Brother Giles returning to his cell.

On the departure of King Louis, one of the friars asked another of his companions who it was who had remained so long embracing Brother Giles. When he told this to the others they were very upset that Brother Giles had not said a single word to him, and complained saying: 'O Brother Giles, why were you so discourteous that you did not say a single word to so holy a king, who had travelled from France to see you and receive good counsel from you?'

'My dearest brothers,' replied Brother Giles, 'don't be surprised at this; I was unable to say a word to him, nor he to me. For as soon as we embraced each other, the light of divine wisdom revealed and opened his heart to me, and mine to him, so that by looking into each other's hearts, we understood what I wished to say to him and he to me far more clearly than if we had spoken with our mouths. And we received far greater consolation, for if we had to explain in words what we felt in our hearts, we should have been discouraged rather than consoled because of the inadequacy of human language, which is incapable of expressing clearly the hidden mysteries of God. Moreover, you are well aware that the king went away wonderfully comforted.'

CHAPTER 34: *How, during a grave illness, Saint Clare was miraculously transported from her cell to the church*

SAINT CLARE was once seriously ill, so that she could not go to say the Office in church with the other nuns. And on the feast of Christ's Nativity, all the other sisters went to Matins, but she remained in bed, very grieved that she could not go with the others and receive spiritual comfort. But Jesus Christ her Spouse, not willing to leave her thus deprived of consolation, caused her to be miraculously transported by angels to Saint Francis's church, where she remained throughout the Office of Matins and the Midnight Mass. She also received Holy Communion, and afterwards He caused her to be carried back to her bed.

When the nuns came back to Saint Clare after the Office in San Damiano was ended, they said to her: 'O Mother, Sister Clare, what comfort we have received on this holy night of Christ's Nativity! If only it had pleased God that you had been with us!'

And Saint Clare replied: 'Praise and thanks be to my Lord Jesus Christ the Blessed, my sisters and dearest daughters. For I was present at all the solemnities of this most holy night, with great comfort to my soul, and I received even greater comfort than you. At the intercession of my father Saint Francis and by God's grace I myself was present in the church of our Father Saint Francis, and I heard all the singing and the music of the organ with my bodily eyes as well as with my spiritual senses. So for this great favour granted me I praise and thank our Lord Jesus Christ.'

CHAPTER 35: *How Brother Leo had a fair and wondrous vision, and how Saint Francis interpreted it*

SAINT FRANCIS was once seriously ill, and Brother Leo was looking after him. And while Brother Leo was at prayer close to Saint Francis, he entered into ecstasy and was carried away in spirit to a great river, broad and swift. And as he stood to watch what would happen, he saw some friars carrying burdens enter the river, and they were immediately swept away by the force of the water and drowned. Others advanced a third of the distance across, some got as far as the middle, and some nearly reached the further bank; but at length all of them fell and were drowned by the force of the current and because of the loads they were bearing on their backs.

As he watched, Brother Leo was filled with the deepest pity, and while he stood there a great company of friars appeared bearing no burdens of any kind, and in them shone the light of holy poverty. And these entered the river and crossed over without any danger. And when he had seen this, Brother Leo returned to himself.

Then Saint Francis, knowing in spirit that Brother Leo had seen a vision of some kind, called him to him and asked him what he had seen. And when Brother Leo had described the vision in due order, Saint Francis said: 'What you have seen is true. The great river is this world; the friars who were drowned in the river are those who have not followed the gospel way of life, especially as regards complete poverty. But those who passed over without danger are those friars who neither seek nor possess anything worldly or carnal in this life, and are content to follow Christ naked on the Cross with only the barest necessities of food and clothing. They bear the burden and sweet yoke of Christ and of holy obedience gladly and willingly, and so pass easily from the life of this world to life eternal.'

CHAPTER 36: *How Saint Francis visited the house of a courteous gentleman who was generous with his possessions; and how he became a friar and attained perfection*

SAINT FRANCIS, the servant of God, arrived late one night at the house of a great and influential gentleman, and both he and his companion were made welcome and lodged there with the greatest courtesy and respect as though they were angels from Paradise. In consequence Saint Francis was moved to a great love for this gentleman, when he considered how he had embraced and kissed them lovingly when they entered the house, and how he had humbly washed, dried, and kissed their feet, lit a great fire, and prepared the table with plenty of good food. And while they were eating, he waited on them continually with a happy face.

Now when Saint Francis and his companion had eaten, this gentleman said: 'See, Father, I offer you myself and all my goods. Whenever you need a habit or a cloak or anything whatsoever, buy them and I will pay. And remember that I am willing to provide for all your needs, for by the grace of God I am able to do this, seeing that I have an abundance of worldly possessions. So for the love of God, who has bestowed them on me, I will gladly do good to His poor.'

Saint Francis, seeing so much courtesy and benevolence in him, and appreciating the generosity of his offer, conceived such a love for him that when he left he said to his companion as they walked: 'That gentleman would indeed make a good member of our company, because he is so grateful to God, and so kind and courteous to his neighbour and the poor. Know, my dearest brother, that courtesy is one of the attributes of God, who in His courtesy gives sun and rain to the just and the unjust alike. And courtesy is the sister of charity, which quenches hatred and preserves love. And I have observed so much divine virtue in this good man, that I would like to have him as a companion. So I wish to return to him some day, for God may touch his heart and give him the desire to go with us in God's service. Meanwhile we will pray God to put this desire into his heart, and give him grace to carry it into effect.'

Wonderful to relate, a few days after Saint Francis had made this prayer, God implanted this desire in that gentleman's heart. And Saint Francis said to his companion: 'My brother, let us go to that courteous man, for I have a firm trust in God that he will give himself to us as our companion with the same courtesy that he shows in worldly matters.' So they set out, and as they approached his house Saint Francis said to his companion: 'Wait here a little while, for I will first ask God to prosper our journey, and that it may please Jesus Christ to grant us, poor and weak as we are, to snatch our intended prey from the world by the merits of His most holy Passion.' And so saying, he began to pray in a place where he could be seen by this courteous gentleman.

So it pleased God that as this gentleman was looking around him, he saw Saint Francis engaged in devout prayer before Christ, who appeared to him in great glory as he prayed, and stood before him. And as the gentleman stood where he was, he saw that Saint Francis was raised bodily from the ground for a considerable while. At this sight he was so touched by God and so strongly moved to leave the world that he immediately came out of his palace, and ran towards Saint Francis in great fervour of spirit. And reaching him while he was still at prayer, he knelt down at his feet and begged most insistently and devoutly that he would be pleased to allow him to do penance in his company.

When Saint Francis saw that God had answered his prayer and that the gentleman was asking with great persistence for what he himself desired, he rose in fervour and joy of spirit and he embraced and kissed him, devoutly thanking God who had added so outstanding a knight to his company. Then the gentleman said to Saint Francis: 'What do you wish me to do, my Father? See, I am ready to obey your command, and to give all I possess to the poor, and follow Christ with you unhampered by worldly things.' This he did, and at Saint Francis's direction and advice he distributed all that he possessed among the poor. And he entered the Order, living in great penitence, holiness, and virtue of life. And at his death he entered the glory of the blessed.

CHAPTER 37: *How Saint Francis revealed that Brother Elias was damned; and how, when that brother amended his ways, Saint Francis prayed for him, and he was saved*

SAINT FRANCIS and Brother Elias were once staying in the same Friary, when it was revealed to Saint Francis by God that Brother Elias was damned, and would apostasize from the Order and finally die outside it. Because of this Saint Francis felt so strong an aversion for him that he could not speak or converse with him. If Brother Elias happened to approach him at any time, he used to turn away and go elsewhere to avoid meeting him. Consequently Brother Elias began to realize that Saint Francis was displeased with him. So, wishing to learn the reason, he stopped Saint Francis one day in order to speak to him, and, when Saint Francis turned away, Brother Elias detained him gently but forcibly, and asked him with diffidence to be so kind as to reveal the reason why he avoided his company and refused to speak to him.

Then Saint Francis answered: 'The reason is this; it has been revealed to me by God that because of your sins you will apostasize from the Order and die outside it. And God has also revealed to me that you are damned.' When he heard this, Brother Elias replied: 'My reverend Father, I beg you for the love of God not to shun me on this account or drive me away from you, but as a good shepherd and disciple of Christ recover the sheep that will perish without your aid. And pray God for me, that if it be possible, He may revoke my sentence of damnation; for the Scriptures say that God will revoke the sentence if the sinner repents his sin and amends. I have such faith in your prayers that, were I in the depths of hell and you prayed to God on my behalf, I would feel some comfort. Sinner as I am, therefore I beg you once again to recommend me to Christ who came to save sinners, that He may admit me to His mercy.'

Brother Elias spoke with great devotion and tears, so, as a

loving father, Saint Francis promised to pray for him, and did so. And while he was praying very earnestly on his behalf, he understood by revelation that his prayer had been heard by God, to the extent that Brother Elias's sentence of damnation had been revoked and his soul would not finally be damned; but he would certainly desert the Order and die outside it. And so it came about, for when Frederick, King of Sicily, rebelled against the Church and was excommunicated by the Pope, together with all who had helped or advised him, the said Brother Elias – who was reputed to be one of the cleverest men in the world – went over to King Frederick at his invitation, and in so doing became a rebel against the Church and an apostate from the Order. For this offence he was excommunicated by the Pope, and deprived of the habit of Saint Francis.

While Brother Elias was thus excommunicate, he fell seriously ill, and one of the friars, a lay-brother who had remained in the Order and was a man of good and honest life, learning of his illness, went to visit him. And after talking of other matters, he said to him: 'Dearest brother, it grieves me greatly that you are excommunicated and expelled from your Order, and that you should die in this state. But if you can suggest any way or means by which I can save you from this peril, I will willingly go to any trouble.'

Brother Elias replied: 'My brother, I can see no other way except that you go to the Pope, and beg him for the love of God and of Saint Francis His servant, through whose teaching I renounced the world, to absolve me from excommunication and restore the religious habit to me.' The brother said that he would gladly undertake this task for his salvation, and taking leave of him, he went on foot to the Holy Father, and begged him most humbly to grant this favour to his brother for the love of God and Saint Francis. And, as it pleased God, the Pope consented that the friar should return, and if he found Brother Elias still living, should absolve him on his behalf and restore the habit to him. So he went away gladly, and returned in great haste to Brother Elias, whom he found yet living but very near to death, and he absolved him from excommunication. And having resumed the habit, Brother Elias passed from this life, and his soul found mercy through the merits of Saint Francis and his prayers, in which Brother Elias had placed such great trust.

CHAPTER 38: *How Saint Antony of Padua preached under the inspiration of divine grace, and how men of many races each understood what he said, each in his own language*

THAT wonderful vessel of the Holy Spirit, Saint Antony of Padua, one of the chosen disciples and companions of Saint Francis, who used to call him his bishop, once preached in Consistory before the Pope and Cardinals. Men of different nations were present at this Consistory – Greeks, Latins, French, Germans, Slavs, English, and men of other different languages. And Saint Antony, fired by the Holy Spirit, preached the word of God so convincingly and profoundly, with such clarity and brilliance, that all in the Consistory, although they spoke different languages, understood everything that he said clearly and accurately, as though he had spoken in their own native tongues. And they were all astonished, and it seemed to them a renewal of the ancient miracle at the time of Pentecost, when under the influence of the Holy Spirit the Apostles had spoken in every tongue. And they said to one another with great wonder: 'Does not this preacher come from Spain? How is it that each of us hears the language of his own country as he speaks?' The Pope also, as he considered and admired the profoundness of his preaching, said: 'This friar is indeed the ark of the Testament and the armoury of Holy Scripture.'

CHRIST THE BLESSED willed to display the great holiness of His most faithful servant Saint Antony of Padua, and show how devoutly his preaching and holy doctrine were to be listened to. So on one occasion He rebuked the stupidity of unbelievers and heretics by means of fishes, creatures without reason, just as in the Old Testament He had rebuked the ignorance of Balaam through the mouth of an ass.

Being at one time in Rimini where there were a large number of heretics, Saint Antony wished to recall them to the light of true faith and the way of truth. And he often preached to them, and reasoned with them on the Faith of Christ and on Holy Scripture; but they rejected his holy teaching, and were hardened and obstinate, refusing to listen to him at all. So one day, under God's inspiration, Saint Antony went down to the seashore at the mouth of the river. And standing on the bank between the sea and the river, he began to speak to the fishes as a preacher sent by God. And he said: 'Listen to the word of God, you fish of the sea and river, since the faithless heretics disdain to hear it.'

No sooner had he uttered these words than a great shoal of fish approached the shore, large, small, and medium in size, so that such vast numbers had never been seen in the sea or river before. And they all raised their heads from the water and remained attentive, completely still, tame, and orderly; for the smaller fish remained in front close to the shore, the medium-sized fish lay beyond them, and the larger fish lay further out where the water was deeper. And when all the fish were thus disposed in their species and order, Saint Antony solemnly began to preach to them, and said:

'My brothers the fish, it is your duty, according to your own nature, to give thanks to your Creator, who has given you such a noble element in which to dwell, so that you have sweet and salt waters at your choice, and have been given many places of refuge from the storms. When He made you, your generous and kind Creator commanded you to increase and multiply, and gave you His blessing. When the flood covered the earth all other creatures perished, but God preserved you alone from harm. He has given you fins, so that you may swim wherever you will. To you was assigned the duty, under God's command, to preserve the prophet Jonah, and after the third day to cast him ashore safe and sound. It was you who provided the tribute-money for your Lord Jesus Christ, who in His poverty had nothing with which to pay. By a singular mystery you provided food for the Eternal King, Jesus Christ, both before and after His Resurrection. Because of these things you are under a deep obligation to praise and bless God, who has given you blessings above other creatures.'

At these words and counsels of Saint Antony the fish began to open their mouths and bow their heads and, with such other signs of reverence as their nature permitted they gave thanks to God. Then Saint Antony, seeing the great reverence of the fish for their Creator, was glad at heart, and said in a loud voice: 'Blessed be the eternal God, for the fish give greater honour to Him than men who are heretics, and irrational creatures listen to His word with greater attention than men without faith.' And as long as Saint Antony continued to preach, the great shoal of fish grew, and not one of them left the place it had taken.

When this miracle became known the people of the city began to hasten to the shore, dragging the heretics with them. And seeing so wonderful and unmistakable a miracle, they were touched to the heart, and all threw themselves at Saint Antony's feet to listen to his words. Then Saint Antony began to expound the Catholic Faith, and spoke so eloquently that all the heretics were converted and returned to the true faith of Christ. And all the faithful were filled with great joy, and were comforted and confirmed in their holy faith.

After this Saint Antony dismissed the fish with God's blessing, and they all swam away with marvellous movements of joy. The people also went away, and Saint Antony remained in Rimini many days, preaching and gathering in a great spiritual harvest of souls.

CHAPTER 40: *On Brother Simon, who was so holy that he cast out the devil by his prayer, and how he prayed for a sorely tempted friar, and God delivered him*

IN the early days of the Order, during the lifetime of Saint Francis, there entered the Order a young man of Assisi called Brother Simon. And God granted him such grace, such gifts of contemplation, and so devout a mind that his whole life was a mirror of sanctity, as I have heard from those who lived a long time with him. He was very seldom seen outside his cell, and whenever he was with the other friars, he always spoke of God. He had never studied in the schools, but he used to speak of God and prayer to Christ with such deep wisdom and lofty understanding that his words seemed supernatural.

One evening he went into the wood with Brother Jacopo da Massa to talk of God, and they conversed most sweetly on the love of God, and spent the whole night in this way. And as Brother Jacopo himself told me, when morning came it seemed to them that only a short time had passed.

At times of illumination and of the loving visitations of God, this Brother Simon experienced such sweetness and joy in the Holy Spirit that whenever he sensed their coming he often lay down on his bed, for the tranquil joy of the Holy Spirit brought him not only peace of soul but repose of body. And during these visitations by God he often entered into rapture, and became wholly insensible to worldly things.

Once while he was thus rapt in God and dead to the world, he was inwardly aflame with the love of God and completely insensible to bodily feelings. And one of the friars, wishing to test this and discover whether he was as unconscious as he appeared, went and took a live coal and laid it on his bare foot. And Brother Simon felt nothing, neither did it leave any mark on his foot, although it remained there so long that it burned out of itself.

Whenever this Brother Simon took his place at table, before partaking of bodily food, he both received and gave food for the soul by speaking about God. By his devout conversation he once converted a young man of San Severino, who as a layman had been very vain and worldly, being of noble blood and brought up in great luxury. And when Brother Simon received this young man into the Order, he took charge of his secular clothing himself; and the young man remained with Brother Simon to receive instruction in the observance of the Rule. Whereupon the devil, who sets himself to thwart every good intention, tormented him with such strong desires and violent bodily temptations that he was quite unable to withstand them. So he came to Brother Simon and said: 'Give me back my clothes that I wore in the world, for I cannot resist this bodily temptation any longer.' Filled with great compassion for the young man, Brother Simon said: 'Sit down here with me for a little while'; and he proceeded to speak of God in such a way that all temptation left him. And later, when the temptation returned and he demanded his clothes, Brother Simon again dispelled it by talking of God.

This happened on several occasions, and at length the temptation came upon him more violently than ever before, so that he could not resist it for anything in the world; and he went to Brother Simon to demand the return of all his secular clothes, for on no account could he remain any longer. Then Brother Simon made him sit down beside him as he had always done, and as he spoke to him of God, the young man leaned his head on Brother Simon's breast, overcome by despair and grief. Then in deep pity Brother Simon raised his eyes to heaven, and as he prayed God very earnestly for him, the young man fell into ecstasy, and Brother Simon's prayer was heard. And when the young man returned to himself he felt himself completely freed from that temptation as though he had never experienced it. Indeed, once the flame of temptation had been transformed into the fire of the Holy Spirit by contact with Brother Simon that glowing coal, he became wholly afire with the love of God and his neighbour. So great was this transformation that once, when an evil-doer had been arrested and was about to have his eyes put out, this young friar was filled with pity and went boldly to the Governor in full Council, and with many tears and earnest entreaties asked that they should put out one of his own eyes and one of the evil-doer's, in order that the man might not be completely sightless. But the Governor and the Council, recognizing the great fervour and charity of the friar, pardoned them both.

One day while Brother Simon was at prayer in the wood and experiencing deep consolation of soul, a flock of rooks began to disturb him by their cawing. So he ordered them in the name of Jesus to fly away and return no more. And the birds flew away and were never seen or heard again there or in the surrounding district. And this miracle was known throughout the Province of Fermo, in which this friary was situated.

CHAPTER 41: *An account of certain holy friars, and in particular of Brother Conrad and a friar who carried a leper fifteen miles between dawn and sunrise*

THE Province of the March of Ancona was formerly adorned by holy friars as the sky is adorned with stars; like heavenly bodies, these friars illumined and adorned the Order of Saint Francis and the world by their examples and teaching. Among others in the early days was Brother Lucidus Antico, who shone with true holiness and glowed with divine charity; whose glorious tongue, inspired by the Holy Spirit, won marvellous results by his preaching. Another was Brother Bentivoglia of San Severino, who was seen by Brother Masseo of San Severino lifted up in the air for a long while as he prayed in the wood. As a result of this miracle Brother Masseo, who was then a parish priest, resigned his benefice and became a Friar Minor, and attained such sanctity that he performed many miracles both during his lifetime and after his death; and his body rests at Murro.

Once, while this Brother Bentivoglia was staying at Trave Bonanti to look after and nurse a leper, he received an order from his superior to leave that place and go to another about fifteen miles distant. Not wishing to desert the leper, he lifted him up with fervent charity, and, placing him on his shoulders, carried him the entire distance of fifteen miles between dawn and sunrise to the place whither he had been sent, which was called Monte Saracino. Had he been an eagle he could not have completed this journey in so short a time; and this divine miracle caused great wonder and admiration throughout the countryside.

Another was Brother Peter of Monticello, who was seen by Brother Servodio of Urbino, then Guardian of the old friary at Ancona, raised bodily about eight feet above the ground level with the feet of the crucifix before which he was praying. At one time, when Brother Peter had been fasting with great devotion during the forty days' fast of Saint Michael, he was at prayer in the church on the last day of that fast. And he was heard talking with Saint Michael the Archangel by a young friar, who had carefully concealed himself beneath the high altar in order to see some evidence of his sanctity. And their words were as follows: Saint Michael said: 'Peter, you have striven faithfully in my honour, and mortified your body in many ways. See, I have now come to comfort you, so you may ask whatever grace you desire, and I will obtain it for you from God.'

Brother Peter replied: 'Most holy Prince of the heavenly hosts, and most faithful champion of God's honour, gracious protector of souls, I ask this grace – that you obtain for me from God the forgiveness of my sins.'

'Ask some other favour,' answered Saint Michael, 'for I can readily obtain this grace for you.'

And when Brother Peter refused to ask anything further, the Archangel concluded: 'Because of your faith and the devotion that you have to me, I will obtain both the grace for which you have asked and many others as well.' And having ended their conversation, which had continued a long while, the Archangel departed, leaving him greatly comforted.

A contemporary of this holy Brother Peter was Brother Conrad of Offida, who belonged to the same community at the friary of Forano, in the Custody of Ancona. One day this Brother Conrad went out into the wood in order to contemplate and Brother Peter followed him secretly to see what would happen to him. And Brother Conrad began to pray, and with many tears most devoutly begged the Virgin Mary to obtain for him from her blessed Son the grace to experience a little of that joy felt by holy Simeon on the day of the Purification, when he held Jesus our Blessed Saviour in his arms. And when he had made this prayer, the merciful Virgin Mary granted his request; and the Queen of Heaven appeared with her Son in her arms in a great radiance of light, and coming to Brother Conrad she placed her blessed Son in his arms. And he received Him with the deepest reverence, embracing and kissing Him; and he pressed Him to his breast, utterly melted and dissolved by divine love and unspeakable consolation. And when the Virgin Mary left Brother Conrad, Brother Peter returned in haste to the friary lest he should be seen by him; but later, when Brother Conrad returned overcome with joy and gladness, Brother Peter said to him: 'O heavenly soul, how great a consolation has been yours!'

'What are you saying, Brother Peter?' answered Brother Conrad. 'What do you know about what I have received?'

'I know well,' said Brother Peter, 'I know well that the Virgin Mary with her Son has visited you.' Then Brother Conrad, who was truly humble and wished to conceal the graces granted him by God, begged him not to speak of it to anyone. And from that time there existed so great a love between them that they seemed to have one heart and one soul in all things.

Once at the friary of Sirolo this same Brother Conrad by his prayers delivered a woman possessed by a devil. He prayed for her all night, and after seeing her mother he left in haste next morning lest he should be found and honoured by the people.

CHAPTER 42: *How Brother Conrad converted an obstinate friar with great charity, so that he forthwith became the most perfect friar in the house*

THIS Brother Conrad of Offida, who was full of zeal for evangelical poverty and the Rule of Saint Francis, was a man of so religious a life and such great merit before God that Christ the Blessed honoured him by many miracles, both during his life and after his death. Amongst these, once when he was visiting the friary at Offida as a guest the brethren begged him for love of God and of charity to admonish a young friar who behaved in so childish, careless, and disorderly a way that he disturbed both young and old in the community, and paid little or no attention to the Divine Office and other observances of the Rule.

So out of pity for the young man and in response to the request of the other friars, Brother Conrad called the young man aside, and with ardent charity gave him such effective and devout counsel that, under the influence of God's grace, he changed forthwith from a child into an older man in his behaviour. And he became so obedient and gentle, considerate and devout – and in due course so peaceable and helpful, so zealous in every virtue – that whereas at first the entire community had been disturbed by him, so now all were content and happy, and loved him very much.

As it pleased God, it came about that soon after his conversion this young man died, and the friars were very grieved. And shortly after his death, his soul appeared to Brother Conrad as he was praying devoutly before the altar of the friary, and addressed him respectfully as 'Father'. And Brother Conrad asked: 'Who are you?'

To which he replied: 'I am the soul of that young friar who died the other day.'

And Brother Conrad said: 'My dearest son, how is it with you?'

And he answered: 'Dearest Father, by the grace of God and as a result of your instruction, it is well, in so far that I am not damned: but because of my sins, for which I had no time to make sufficient expiation, I am suffering very severe pains in Purgatory. But I beg you, Father, that as of your pity you helped me when I was living, so now it may please you to ease me in my pains by saying the *Our Father* for me several times, for your prayer is very acceptable in the sight of God.'

Then Brother Conrad gladly assented to his request, and

said an *Our Father* and *Rest Eternal;* whereupon the soul said: 'O dearest Father, how great a benefit and relief I feel! I beg you, say it once again.' And Brother Conrad said it; and when he had done so, the soul said: 'Holy Father, when you pray for me, I feel completely at ease, so I beg you not to cease praying for me.' And when Brother Conrad saw how greatly the soul was helped by his prayers, he said an hundred *Our Fathers* for him. And when he had ended, the soul said: 'Dearest Father, I thank you in the name of God for the charity you have shown me, for by your prayer you have delivered me from all my pains, and I am going to the heavenly kingdom.' And with these words, the soul departed. Then Brother Conrad comforted the other friars with great joy, and gave them a full account of the vision.

CHAPTER 43: *How two friars loved each other so deeply that they disclosed all their revelations to one another*

AT one time Brother Conrad and the above Brother Peter lived together in the friary of Forano in the Custody of Ancona. Both were shining stars in the Province of the March, and a pair of heavenly mortals, for there so great a love and charity existed between them that they seemed to possess but one heart and one soul. And they bound themselves together by an agreement that every consolation that the mercy of God granted them they would reveal to one another in charity.

Having made this agreement, it happened one day while Brother Peter was at prayer and meditating on the Passion of Christ, and how the most blessed Mother of Christ and Saint John the best beloved disciple and Saint Francis were depicted at the foot of the Cross, crucified with Christ by mental anguish, there came to him a desire to know which of the three had suffered the greatest grief at the Passion of Christ;

whether the Mother who had borne Him, or the disciple who had rested on His heart, or Saint Francis who had been crucified with the wounds of Christ. And as he was devoutly meditating on these matters, the Virgin Mary appeared to him with Saint John the Evangelist and Saint Francis, clothed in the noblest robes of blessed glory; but Saint Francis seemed to be clothed in even more beautiful robes than Saint John.

And as Brother Peter stood awestruck at this vision, Saint John comforted him and said: 'Have no fear, dearest brother, for we are come to comfort you and set you free from uncertainty. Know, therefore, that the Mother of Christ and I felt greater grief at the Passion of Christ than all other creatures; but next to us Saint Francis felt a greater grief than any other, and that is why you see him in such glory.'

And Brother Peter asked him: 'Most holy Apostle of Christ, why does the robe of Saint Francis appear more beautiful than your own?'

'The reason is this,' replied Saint John, 'that while he lived on earth he wore more wretched garments than I did.' And with these words Saint John handed Brother Peter a gorgeous robe that he was carrying in his hand, and said: 'Take this robe which I have brought to give you.' And when Saint John wished to clothe him in it, Brother Peter fell to the ground in amazement, and began to cry out: 'Brother Conrad! Dearest Brother Conrad! Help me quickly! Come and see a marvellous thing!' And as he spoke, the vision disappeared. Then when Brother Conrad came, he described all that had happened, and they thanked God.

CHAPTER 44: *How a certain friar, while still a boy in the world, was miraculously called by God to join the Order*

WHILE Brother John of Penna was still a boy living in the world in the Province of the March, a very lovely Child appeared to him one night and called him, saying: 'John, go to Saint Stephen's, where one of My friars is preaching. Pay attention to his teaching and listen to his words, for I have sent him. When you have done this, you must go on a long journey, and then you shall come to Me.' At this, the boy immediately got up, feeling a great change within his soul.

And he went to Saint Stephen's, and found a large crowd of men and women gathered there to hear the sermon, and the man about to preach was Brother Philip, one of the first friars to visit the March of Ancona, for at that time there were few friars in the March. Then Brother Philip stood up to preach, and spoke with the greatest devotion, proclaiming the kingdom of everlasting life not with words of human wisdom but with the power of the Spirit. And when the sermon was ended, the boy went to Brother Philip and said: 'Father, if you are willing to receive me into the Order, I will gladly do penance and serve our Lord Jesus Christ.' As he looked at the boy and recognized his wonderful innocence and eagerness to serve God, Brother Philip said to him: 'Come to me on a certain day at Recanati, and I will have you received,' for it was here that the Provincial Chapter was about to be held.

When he heard this, the boy, who was very simple, imagined that this was the long journey that he was to make according to the revelation he had received, and that he would then go to heaven; and he thought that this would happen as soon as he had been received into the Order. When he found that his expectation was not to be fulfilled, and hearing the Minister say in Chapter that he would gladly grant permission to anyone who wished to go to the Province of Provence, he felt a strong desire to go there, believing in his heart that this would be the long journey that he had to make before he entered heaven. But being too shy to mention it, he at length confided in Brother Philip, who had him received into the Order, and lovingly asked him to obtain for him the favour of going to the Province of Provence. Then Brother Philip, knowing his purity and good intention, obtained this permission for him. So Brother John made ready to leave with great joy, having a firm conviction that when he had completed his journey he would go to heaven. But it pleased God that he should remain in that Province for twenty-five years, holding to that hope and desire, and showing himself a pattern of sincerity and holiness. He constantly increased in virtue, and in the favour of God and the people, and was greatly beloved by friars and layfolk alike.

One day, as Brother John was praying with devotion, weeping and sorrowing because his longing had not been fulfilled and his pilgrimage in this life had been so prolonged, Christ the Blessed appeared to him. At the sight of Him his soul wholly melted within him, and Christ said to him: 'My son, Brother John, ask of Me whatever you will.'

And he answered: 'My Lord, I do not know what to ask except Yourself, for I desire nothing else. My sole request is that You pardon my sins and grant me grace to see You another time when I shall have greater need.'

Christ said: 'Your prayer is granted.' With these words He departed, leaving Brother John wholly consoled and comforted.

At length the friars of the March, hearing of his reputation for holiness, pressed the Minister General so strongly that he ordered Brother John under obedience to return to the March. Brother John gladly obeyed this order and set out on the road, trusting that at the end of his journey he would go to heaven as Christ had promised. But when he had returned to the Province of the March, he lived there for thirty years, and was not recognized by any of his relatives; and day by day he hoped that God in His mercy would fulfil His promise to him. During this time he filled the office of Guardian on several occasions with great discretion, and God worked many miracles through him. And among other gifts he received from God was the gift of prophecy.

Once, when he was away from the friary, one of his novices was assailed by the devil and tempted with such violence that, yielding to the temptation, he made up his mind to leave the Order as soon as Brother John should return. But this temptation and his decision were revealed to Brother John by the spirit of prophecy, and returning to the house at once, he called this novice to him and told him to confess. But before he confessed, Brother John described the whole course of his temptation as God had revealed it to him, and ended by saying: 'My son, because you waited for me and did not wish to go away without my blessing, God has granted you the favour that you will never desert this Order, but will die within it in the grace of God.' Then this novice was strengthened in his good resolution, and he remained in the Order and became a holy friar. And all these events are related by me, Brother Ugolino.

This Brother John was a man of a happy and quiet disposition; he seldom spoke, and was given to deep devotion and prayer, especially after Matins, when he never used to return to his cell to sleep, but would remain in prayer in the church till dawn. And one night as he was praying after Matins, the angel of God appeared to him and said: 'Brother John, your life is drawing to its close, as you have desired for so long. God has sent me to tell you that you may choose whichever favour you wish, either one day in Purgatory or seven days suffering in this world.' And when Brother John chose seven days of suffering in this world, he forthwith fell ill with various ailments. He was attacked by a high fever, by gout in hands and feet, by a pain in the side, and by many other ills. But the worst of all his afflictions was a devil who stood constantly before him holding in his hand a great scroll inscribed with all the sins he had committed, and saying: 'For these sins that you have committed in thought, word, and deed you are damned to the depths of hell.' And he could not recall any good that he had done, nor that he belonged to the Order or ever had, but thought himself damned as the devil said. So whenever he was asked how he did, he replied: 'Badly, for I am damned.'

When the friars saw his condition they were amazed, and sent for an old friar named Brother Matthew of Monte Rubbiano, a holy man and a close friend of Brother John. And Brother Matthew came to him on the seventh day of his sufferings, and asked how he did. And he answered that things went badly for him, because he was damned. Then Brother Matthew said: 'Don't you remember how you have often confessed to me, and how I have given you full absolution for your sins? And don't you remember how you have served God in this holy Order for very many years? Furthermore, don't you remember that the mercy of God is greater than all the sins of the world, and that Christ our blessed Saviour paid an infinite price to redeem us? So have good hope that you are assuredly saved.'

As he spoke the period of Brother John's afflictions drew to an end, the temptation departed, and consolation came to him. And Brother John said to Brother Matthew with great joy: 'You are tired and the hour is late; I beg you, go and rest.' Brother Matthew did not wish to leave him, but at length yielded to his insistence, and went away to lie down. And Brother John remained alone with the friar who was tending him. And Christ the Blessed came in great splendour with the sweetest fragrance to fulfil His promise to appear to him on another occasion when he should have the greater need. And He healed him completely of all his infirmities.

Then Brother John folded his hands and thanked God that he had reached such a perfect ending to his long journey through this present life of sorrow. And he gave up his soul into the hands of Christ, passing from this mortal life to life everlasting with Christ the Blessed, whom he had so long desired and awaited. And Brother John rests in the friary at Penna.

CHAPTER 45: *How a certain friar saw the soul of his brother, also a friar, ascend to heaven, and how he paid reverence to his remains*

In the above Province of the March, after the death of Saint Francis, there were two brothers in the Order; one was named Brother Humilis and the other Brother Pacificus, and both were men of great holiness and perfection. The former, Brother Humilis, belonged to the friary at Soffiano, where he also died; the latter belonged to another friary a considerable distance away. One day it pleased God that Brother Pacificus, who was at prayer in a lonely place, should be caught up into ecstasy, and he saw the soul of his brother Humilis ascend direct to heaven without any delay or difficulty at the moment it left his body.

After many years it happened that this Brother Pacificus, who still survived, was transferred to the community in this friary at Soffiano where his brother had died. At this juncture the friars were moving from this friary to another at the request of the Lords of Brunforte, and in consequence they took away with them, among other things, the remains of the holy friars who had died in this house. And coming to the grave of Brother Humilis, his own brother, Brother Pacificus took up his bones, washed them in good wine, and wrapped them in a napkin. And he kissed them and wept over them with great reverence and devotion.

The other friars were scandalized at this, and considered such behaviour improper, for although Brother Pacificus was a man of great holiness, he seemed to mourn his brother with a sentimental and worldly love, and to show greater respect to his remains than to those of the other friars, who had been no less holy than Brother Humilis and deserved equal reverence.

Realizing the critical feelings of the other friars, Brother Pacificus humbly carried out their wishes, and said: 'My dearest brothers, don't be surprised if I have done more for the bones of my own brother than for the others, for – blessed be God – I was not moved by human affection as you imagine. I acted in this way because when my brother passed from this life, I was praying in a lonely place, and although I was far away from him, I saw his soul ascend direct to heaven. So I am sure that his bones are holy, and that he must be in Paradise. And if God had given me the same certainty with regard to the other friars, I would have paid the same reverence to their bones.' So when the friars realized the devotion and holiness of his intention, they were very edified, and praised God who has done such wonderful things in His saints.

CHAPTER 46: *How the Virgin Mary brought three boxes of electuary* to a friar who was mortally ill, and healed him*

IN the same friary of Soffiano there formerly lived a Friar Minor of such holiness and grace that he seemed altogether spiritual, and was often caught up into God. This friar, who was pre-eminently endowed with the gift of contemplation, was once so completely absorbed and uplifted in God that many kinds of birds flew to him and alighted tamely on his head and shoulders, arms and hands, and broke into marvellous song. He was a great lover of solitude and seldom spoke, but whenever he was asked any question, he used to reply with such grace and wisdom that he seemed an

---

* A mixture or paste of medicinal ingredients, usually compounded in honey or sugar.

angel rather than a man. And he was a great contemplative and man of prayer, so that the friars held him in high reverence.

As this friar drew near to the close of his holy life, in accordance with God's will, he fell mortally sick so that he could take nothing to drink. Nor would he take any medicine for the body, but placed his entire trust in the heavenly physician, Jesus Christ the Blessed and His blessed Mother. And because of this he was worthy, by the clemency of God, to receive a merciful visitation and comfort. So as he lay on his bed and prepared for death with all his heart and with the greatest devotion, the glorious and most blessed Virgin Mary, Mother of Jesus Christ, appeared to him, accompanied by a great host of angels and holy virgins, and approached his bed in marvellous splendour. As he gazed at her, this friar was filled with infinite comfort and joy both of body and soul, and humbly began to pray that she would intercede with her beloved Son, that by His merits He would deliver him from the prison of this wretched body. And as he continued in this petition with many tears, the Virgin Mary answered him, calling him by name, and saying: 'Have no doubts, my son, for He has granted your request, and I am come to comfort you a little before you depart this life.'

Accompanying the Virgin Mary were three holy virgins, who bore in their hands three boxes of electuary of incomparable fragrance and sweetness. Then the glorious Virgin Mary took one of the boxes and opened it, and the whole house was filled with its fragrance. And taking some of the electuary with a spoon, she gave it to the sick man. And as soon as he had tasted it, he experienced such ineffable comfort and sweetness that it seemed that his soul could not remain in his body. So he began to say: 'No more, O sweetest Mother of Jesus Christ, blessed Virgin Mary, refuge of mankind! No more, O blessed healer! No more, for I cannot endure such sweetness.' But the loving and compassionate

Mother continued to administer the electuary to the sick friar until the whole box was empty.

Then having emptied the first box, the Blessed Virgin Mary took the second box and inserted the spoon to administer its contents also. So he said faintly: 'O fairest Mother of God, my soul is almost melted away by the fragrance and sweetness of the first electuary; how can I endure the second? Blessed above all saints and angels, I beg you give me no more.'

Our Lady replied: 'Taste but a little of this second box, my son.' And when she had given him a little, she said: 'Now you have had enough, my son; be comforted, for I shall soon return for you and lead you to the Kingdom of my Son, which you have always sought and desired.' With these words, she took leave of him and departed, leaving him so strengthened and comforted by the sweetness of this medicine that he lived for several days satisfied and strong without taking any bodily food. And after some days, while he was talking happily with the friars, he passed away from this life of sorrow to the life of the blessed with great joy and gladness.

CHAPTER 47: *How a friar remained in ecstasy for three days, and was shown the whole state of the Order and what would happen in the future*

BROTHER JAMES OF MASSA, to whom God opened the door to His secrets and granted perfect knowledge and understanding of Holy Scripture and of things to come, was a man of such sanctity that Brother Giles of Assisi, Brother Mark of Montino, Brother Juniper, and Brother Lucidus said of him that they knew of no one in the world higher in God's favour. I also had a great desire to see this Brother James, for when I asked Brother John, a companion of Brother Giles, to explain a certain spiritual matter to me, he told me: 'If you want to receive direction in the spiritual life, go and consult Brother James of Massa, for Brother Giles once wished to obtain guidance from him, and no one can add to or subtract from anything that he says, for his mind has pierced the mysteries of heaven, and his words are the words of the Holy Spirit: There is no one in the world I want so much to meet as Brother James.'

When Brother John of Parma first became Minister, Brother James was at prayer during Prime when he was caught up into God and remained in ecstasy for three days. While in this state all bodily sensations left him, and he was so deeply unconscious that the friars were not sure whether or not he was dead. And during this ecstasy God revealed to him everything that was to take place in our Order; so when I heard of this, my desire to see and speak with him increased. And when it pleased God that I should have an opportunity to speak with him, I made this request: 'If what I have heard about you is true, I beg you not to keep it from me. I have heard that when you lay as though dead for three days, God revealed to you among other matters all that would happen in our Order. I have been told this by Brother Matthew, the Minister of the March, to whom you revealed it under obedience.' Then Brother James with great humility acknowledged that what Brother Matthew said was true.

And what he said, in the words of Brother Matthew, Minister of the March, is as follows: 'I know a friar to whom God has revealed all that will happen to our Order. For Brother James of Massa disclosed to me that, after many matters which God revealed to him about the state of the Church Militant, he saw in a vision a great and beautiful tree, whose roots were of gold, its fruits were men, and all were Friars Minor. Its main branches were distinct, and corresponded to the number of Provinces in the Order, and each branch bore as many friars as belonged to the respective Provinces represented by that branch. In this way he knew the total number of all the friars in the Order and in each Province, their names, state, and condition, their office, rank, and dignity, and the merits and faults of them all. And he saw Brother John of Parma on the highest tip of the branch at the centre of the tree, and on the tips of other branches springing from the centre of the tree stood the Ministers of all the Provinces.

After this he saw Christ seated on a lofty shining throne, and He summoned Saint Francis and gave him a chalice brimming with life, and sent him forth, saying: 'Go and visit your friars, and give them to drink from this chalice the spirit of life. For the spirit of Satan will rise up against them and assail them, and many of them will fall and be unable to rise again.' And Christ gave Saint Francis two angels to accompany him.

Then Saint Francis came to offer the chalice of life to his friars, and he gave it first of all to Brother John, who took it and drained it swiftly and devoutly; and forthwith he became all radiant as the sun. Then Saint Francis offered it to all the other friars in turn, and those who received it with fitting reverence and devotion and drank all of it became glorious as the sun. All those who spilled it and received it without devotion became black and dark, deformed and horrible to see, while those who drank part and wasted part became partly shining and partly dark, either more or less according to the amount of the drink that they had received or wasted. But Brother John, who had drained the chalice of life more fully, shone more brightly than all the others, and by this means he was enabled to gaze into the infinite depths of the light of God. And in so doing he learned of the trouble and tempest that was to rise against this tree, and shake and batter its branches.

So Brother John left the top of the tree where he was standing, and descending through all the branches, concealed himself on firm ground at the roots of the tree, and remained there wrapt in thought. Then Brother Bonaventura,* who had drunk part of the chalice and wasted part, climbed up to the branch to the place which Brother John had left. And as he stood there, the nails of his hands became sharp talons of iron, keen as razors. And he left the place to which he had climbed, and tried to hurl himself on Brother John with violence and fury to wound him. But when he saw him, Brother John cried out aloud and commended himself to Christ, who sat upon the throne, and at his call Christ summoned Saint Francis, and handed him a sharp flint-stone, saying: 'Take this stone and cut off Brother Bonaventura's talons with which he seeks to wound Brother John, so that he cannot harm him.' Then Saint Francis went and did as Christ had commanded him. And when he had done this a great storm of wind arose and shook the tree with such violence that the friars fell to the ground. And the first to fall were those who had wasted all the chalice of the spirit of life; and they were carried away by devils to a dismal place of penance. But Brother John and the others who had drained the whole chalice were borne up by angels to a place of life and everlasting light, blessedness, and splendour.

In this vision Brother James saw and recognized each of these friars clearly and distinctly, his name, office, and condition. And the storm beat with such violence against the tree that it fell, and the wind carried it away. Then, as soon as the storm ceased, another tree entirely of gold sprang from its roots, which were also of gold, and this tree produced

---

* Too much should not be made of this savage attack on Bonaventura, who was regarded as the evil genius of the Order by the 'Spiritual' writer of this chapter. Like many men of moderate and pacific policy, he was attacked by both wings of the Order; by the 'Spirituals' for compromising the literal observance of poverty which obtained in the first years of the Order before its rapid growth in numbers, and by the friars of the outlook of Brother Elias, who wished to adapt the Rule of the Order to what they considered to be the needs of the day.

flowers and fruit. About this tree, its growth, its deep roots, its beauty, and its virtue it is better to remain silent than to speak at the present time.

CHAPTER 48: *An account of the venerable Brother John of La Verna, and of the many graces he received from God*

AMONG the other wise and holy fathers and brothers of Saint Francis, who, in the words of Solomon, are the glory of their Father, there lived in our own time in the Province of the March the venerable and saintly Brother John of Fermo, who became known as Brother John of La Verna, in which place he departed this life. He was an outstanding man, and of great holiness.

While still a boy living in the world, this Brother John longed with all his heart for the life of penance, which preserves the purity both of soul and body. Accordingly, even as a little boy, he began to wear a breastplate of mail and a band of iron next the flesh, and to practise severe fasting. In particular, while he was living with the canons of Saint Peter of Fermo, who lived in great luxury, he used to shun bodily pleasures and mortify the body with the strictest abstinence. But his companions were strongly opposed to these practices, and took away his breastplate and hindered his fasting in various ways. God then inspired him with the resolve to leave the world and those who love it, and to surrender himself unreservedly into the arms of the Crucified by taking the habit of Saint Francis who bore the wounds of the Crucified; and this he did.

Having been received into the Order as a boy and entrusted to the care of the Novice-Master, he grew up so spiritual and devout that whenever he listened to his master speaking of God his heart melted like wax before the fire. And he used to be so overcome with delight by the grace and love of God that he could not bear to sit still in one place while experiencing such sweetness, but rose like one intoxicated in spirit and ran about the garden, the wood, or the church as the fire and ardour of the Spirit moved him.

In the course of time the grace of God enabled this angelic man to make steady progress from virtue to virtue, to attain heavenly gifts, and to enter into ecstasy, so that his mind was at one time uplifted to the glories of the Cherubim, at another to the burning love of the Seraphim, to the glories of the Blessed, or to the loving and ineffable embrace of Christ Himself. And he experienced these things not only inwardly and spiritually, but with actual physical sensations. On one especial and notable occasion the fire of divine love set his heart aflame, and this fire continued to burn within him for three whole years, during which he received marvellous consolation and enlightenment from God, entered into contemplation and rapture, and was visited by God. He was often absorbed in God, and for a short while during this period he appeared wholly aflame and burning with the love of Christ, and this took place on the sacred mountain of La Verna.

But since God has an especial care for His children, giving them at one time consolation, at another tribulation, at another prosperity, at another adversity, according to whatever He sees to be needful to preserve them in humility or to inspire them to a greater love of heavenly things, it pleased God in His goodness after three years to take away this light and fire of divine love from Brother John, and to deprive him of all spiritual comfort. So Brother John was left without the light and love of God, utterly disconsolate and full of grief. Because of this loss he went into the wood and ran to and fro in his anguish, calling aloud with moans and sighs to the beloved Spouse of his soul, who had withdrawn and hidden Himself from him, and without whose presence his soul could find neither peace nor rest. But nowhere and in no way could he find his sweet Jesus, nor could he rediscover the spiritual joys of the love of Christ that he formerly enjoyed. This distress continued for many days, during which he continued with tears and sighs to implore God in His mercy to restore to him the beloved Spouse of his soul.

At length, when it pleased God to have made sufficient trial of his patience and increased his longing for Jesus, one day Brother John was walking through the wood distressed and troubled. And in his weariness he came to a beech-tree and sat down, remaining there gazing up to heaven with his face bathed in tears. Suddenly Jesus Christ appeared to him on the path by which Brother John had come, but He did not speak. When Brother John saw Him, he knew without doubt that it was Christ, and at once flung himself at His feet, begging Him very humbly and with many tears: 'Help me, my Lord, for without Thee, my Saviour, I dwell in darkness and grief. Without Thee, gentle Lamb of God, I live in pain and fear; without Thee, Son of God most High, I live in confusion and disgrace. Without Thee I am deprived of all good and blinded, for Thou art the Life of souls and Life of life. Without Thee I am barren and dry, for Thou art the Source of every good gift and every grace. Without Thee I am utterly desolate, for Thou art Jesus, our Redeemer, our love, and our desire, the Bread of comfort and Wine that gladdens the hearts of Angels and of all the Saints. Give me light, most gracious Master and most tender Shepherd, for I am Thy little sheep, unworthy as I am.'

But because, when God delays its fulfilment, the longing of the saints is kindled to even greater love and merit, Christ the Blessed went away along the path by which He had come without granting his request or answering him a word. Then Brother John got up and ran after Him, throwing himself at His feet once more, and detaining Him with reverent importunity. And he begged Him with fervent tears, saying: 'O sweetest Jesus, have pity on my misery! Hear me in the abundance of Thy mercy, and by the truth of Thy salvation restore to me the joy of Thy face and look kindly on me, for the whole earth is full of Thy mercy.' But Christ passed on once again, and neither spoke to him nor gave him any comfort. But He was acting as a mother towards her little child when she wants it to take the breast, and allows it to follow her crying, so that it will take it more eagerly. Accordingly Brother John followed Christ with even greater fervour and desire, and as he came up with Him, Christ the Blessed turned and gazed at him gladly and graciously; and opening His holy and merciful arms, He embraced him very tenderly. And as Christ opened His arms, Brother John saw issuing from the Saviour's most sacred breast rays of wondrous light, which illumined the whole wood and himself as well, both in soul and body.

Then Brother John prostrated himself at the feet of Christ, and Blessed Jesus, as He did to Magdalen, graciously allowed him to kiss His foot. And Brother John, clasping it with the deepest reverence, bathed it with so many tears that he seemed another Magdalen indeed. And he said with fervour: 'I beg Thee, my Lord, regard not my sins, but by Thy most holy Passion and the shedding of Thy precious Blood, restore my soul to the grace of Thy love; for it is Thy command that we should love Thee with all our heart and all our love, and we cannot fulfil this commandment without Thy help. Help me, then, most blessed Son of God, so that I may love Thee with all my heart and with all my strength.'

And as Brother John prayed thus at the feet of Jesus Christ, his prayer was heard, and he regained his former state of grace, that is, the flame of divine love, and he felt himself fully restored and comforted. And realizing that the gift of divine grace had been restored to him, he began to thank Christ the Blessed, and to kiss His feet. Then, as he raised himself to gaze on the Saviour's face, Christ stretched out His most holy hands and gave them him to kiss. And when Brother John had kissed them, he drew nearer and leaned on

Jesus's breast; and he embraced and kissed Him, and Christ also embraced and kissed Brother John. And during this embrace and kiss Brother John became aware of so heavenly a fragrance that if all the spices and scents of the whole world had been melted into one, it would have seemed a mere stench in comparison to this fragrance. And Brother John was enraptured, consoled, and illumined by this fragrance, which remained in his soul for many months.

Thenceforward his lips, which had drunk at the fount of divine wisdom in the Sacred Heart of the Saviour, uttered wonderful and heavenly words, which touched the hearts of all who heard them and gathered a great harvest of souls. And on that path through the wood where the blessed feet of Christ had rested, and for a considerable distance around, Brother John was always aware of that same fragrance and splendour whenever he passed that way for a long time afterwards.

When Brother John came to himself after his ecstasy and the sacred presence of Christ had been withdrawn, he remained so illumined in soul regarding the mystery of Christ's Divinity, that although he was not a scholarly man by human standards, he wonderfully solved and expounded the most subtle and lofty questions concerning the Holy Trinity, and the profound mysteries of Holy Scripture. And on many occasions afterwards, when speaking before the Pope and Cardinals, and before kings, barons, masters, and doctors, he astonished them by the lofty words and profound truths that he uttered.

CHAPTER 49: *How Brother John said Mass for the souls in Purgatory with such efficacy that God showed him many souls entering Paradise through the merits of that Mass*

ONCE when Brother John was saying Mass on the day after All Saints Day for the souls of all the departed, as the Church has ordered, he offered this most noble Sacrament – which, because of its efficacy, the souls of the departed desire above all other benefits that can be conferred on them – with such charity and heartfelt compassion that he appeared to be wholly melted by the sweetness of his pity and brotherly love. So as he devoutly elevated the Body of Christ during this Mass, offering It to God the Father, and praying that for the love of His blessed Son Jesus Christ, Who hung upon the Cross to redeem our souls, it would please Him to deliver the souls of the departed, whom He had created and redeemed, from the pains of Purgatory, he saw immediately an almost countless host of souls ascend out of Purgatory like a cloud of fiery sparks springing from a burning furnace. And he saw them ascend to heaven through the merits of Christ's Passion, which is daily pleaded for the living and the departed in this most sacred Host, worthy to be adored for ever and ever.

CHAPTER 50: *How, as Brother John was praying for a sick friar, it was revealed to him that the man would die and go to heaven; and how he told him*

AT the time when Brother James of Fallerone, a man of great holiness, was dangerously ill in the friary of Mogliano in the Custody of Fermo, Brother John of La Verna, who was then living in the friary of Massa, heard of his illness. And because he loved him as a dear father, he began to pray for him, devoutly asking God with all his heart to restore him to bodily health if this were to the good of his soul. And while he was occupied in this devout prayer, he was rapt in ecstasy, and saw a great host of angels and saints in the air above the cell of Brother James in the wood. And they shone with such splendour that all the countryside around was bathed with light. And standing among the angels he saw Brother James, the man for whom he was praying, clothed in white and splendid robes. And he saw among them the holy father Francis, adorned with the sacred stigmata of Christ and with great glory. And he saw and recognized the saintly Brother Lucidus, and Brother Matthew of Monte Rubbiano, and many other friars whom he had never seen or known in this life.

And as Brother John gazed at this blessed company of saints with profound joy, it was revealed to him that the salvation of the sick friar's soul was assured, but that he would die of his illness; he would not, however, enter Paradise immediately after his death because he must first be cleansed awhile in Purgatory. By this revelation Brother John was filled with such joy at the salvation of the friar's soul that he felt no sorrow at his bodily death, but he called to him inwardly with great spiritual joy, saying: 'Brother James, my sweet father! Brother James, my sweet brother! Brother James, companion of the angels and friend of the blessed!' Filled with confidence and joy he returned to himself, and hastily leaving the friary, went to visit Brother James at Mogliano. And finding him so ill that he could hardly speak, he announced to him his bodily death and the salvation and glory of his soul according to the assurance that he had received. At this Brother James was greatly comforted in soul and body, and welcomed him with great joy and a happy smile; and he thanked him for the good news he had brought, and devoutly commended himself to his prayers. Then Brother John earnestly begged him to return after his death and inform him of the state of his soul; and Brother James promised to do this if God were willing. After these words, and as the hour of his passing drew near, Brother James began to recite the passage of the psalm: *In pace in idipsum dormiam et requiescam;** and when he had ended, he passed from this life with a glad and happy face.

After the burial of Brother James, Brother John returned to the friary at Massa and awaited the fulfilment of his promise to return on the day he had appointed. But as he was at prayer that day, Christ appeared to him with a great company of saints and angels, and Brother James was not among them; so Brother John, deeply wondering, commended him fervently to Christ. Then on the following day, while Brother John was praying in the wood, Brother James appeared to him accompanied by angels, glorious and full of joy; and Brother John asked him: 'O father, why did you not return to me on the day you promised?'

And Brother James answered: 'Because I had need of some purification. But at the very hour when Christ appeared to you, and you commended me to Him, Christ heard your prayer and set me free from every pain. Then I appeared to the holy lay-brother James of Massa, who as he served at Mass saw the consecrated Host when the priest elevated It transformed into the most lovely living Child. And I told him, "See, I am going with this Child to the kingdom of everlasting life, which no one can enter without Him." '

With these words Brother James vanished, and went to heaven with all the blessed company of angels, leaving Brother John greatly comforted. This Brother James of Fallerone died on the vigil of Saint James the Apostle in the month of July at the friary of Mogliano, where, through his merits, divine goodness worked many miracles after his death.

* Psalm iv. 9.

BECAUSE this Brother John of La Verna had utterly renounced all worldly and temporal pleasures and comforts, and had placed all his joy and all his hope in God, divine goodness granted him wonderful consolations and revelations, especially on the great festivals of Christ.

Once as the festival of Christ's Nativity was drawing near – a time when he confidently expected to receive consolation from God through the sweet mercy of Jesus – the Holy Spirit put into his soul such great and overpowering love for the charity of Christ, which moved Him to humble Himself to take our human nature, that it seemed to Brother John that his very soul was being drawn out of his body and glowed like a furnace. Unable to endure this inward fire, he was in anguish and great distress, and cried out aloud. And he could not restrain his cry, because of the inrush of the Holy Spirit and the overpowering fervour of his love. And in the same hour that this immeasurable fervour overcame him, there came with it such a strong and sure hope of salvation that for nothing in the world could he have believed that, were he to die at that instant, he would have to pass through Purgatory.

This state of soul lasted for a good six months, although the overpowering fervour was not constant, but came upon him at certain hours of the day. And during this time he often received wonderful visitations and many consolations from God, and at certain times he was rapt in God, as was seen by the friar who first recorded these things. Amongst other occasions, one night he was so exalted and rapt in God that he saw all things in heaven and earth in God their Creator, with all their perfections, grades, and separate orders. Then he understood clearly how every creature represents its Creator, and how God is above and within, without, and behind all His creatures. Later he perceived God as Three Persons, and

Three Persons in one God, and the infinite charity which moved the Son of God to become incarnate in obedience to the Father. And lastly he saw in this vision how there is no other way by which the soul can come to God and have eternal life except through Christ the Blessed, who is the Way, the Truth, and the Life of the soul.

CHAPTER 52: *How Brother John experienced wonderful fervour, and entered into ecstasy when he contemplated the Body of Christ*

WHILE living in the same friary of Mogliano, Brother John had the following wonderful experience, which was related by the friars who were present. During the first night after the octave of Saint Laurence, and within the octave of the Assumption of our Lady, after saying Matins in church with the other friars, Brother John felt the unction of divine grace at work within him. And he went out into the garden to meditate on the Passion of Christ, and to prepare himself with all devotion to celebrate Mass, which it was his turn to sing that morning. And while he was meditating on the words of the consecration of the Body of Christ, *Hoc est Corpus Meum*, and marvelling at the infinite love of Christ, who was not only willing to redeem us by His precious Blood, but also to leave us His glorious Body and Blood to be the food of our souls, he began to glow with such fervour and tender love for the love of sweet Jesus that his soul could no longer endure such ecstasy. And he cried out as though intoxicated in spirit *Hoc est Corpus Meum*, repeating the words over and over again; for as he uttered them he seemed to see Christ the Blessed with the Virgin Mary and a host of angels. And as he conversed with them, the Holy Spirit revealed to him all the profound and exalted mysteries of this most noble Sacrament.

And when dawn came he entered the church in this same fervour of spirit and recollection, still repeating the same words, not thinking that he was heard or seen by anyone; but there was a certain friar praying in the church who saw and heard everything. Overcome by this fervour he could not restrain himself because of the abundance of divine grace, and he cried out in a loud voice and continued to do so until the hour of Mass. Then he went to prepare himself and went to the altar.

Having begun the Mass, the further he proceeded the stronger grew the love of Christ and the fervour of devotion, through which he was granted an overwhelming sense of God's presence, which he could neither comprehend nor express in words. So, fearing lest this fervour and sense of God's presence should so greatly increase that he would have to discontinue the Mass, he was in considerable perplexity, and did not know what to do, whether to proceed with the Mass or to wait. And because the same thing had happened on other occasions, and our Lord had so tempered this fervour that he had not been compelled to abandon the Mass, and trusting that he would be able to continue as at other times, he decided with great apprehension to proceed. And as he came to the Preface of our Lady, the divine illumination and the gracious sweetness of the love of God began to grow so strong within him that when he came to the *Qui pridie* he could hardly endure such delight and sweetness. And having at length reached the act of Consecration and pronounced the first words of Consecration over the Host – that is, *Hoc est* – he was incapable of proceeding further, but continued to repeat the words *Hoc est*. And this was because he saw and felt the presence of Christ with a host of angels, and was unable to endure His Majesty. And he saw that Christ did not enter the Host, and knew that the Host would not be changed into the Body of Christ until he pronounced the remaining words, *Corpus Meum.*

Accordingly, as he stood thus troubled and unable to proceed, the Guardian, together with the other friars and many layfolk who were in the church to hear Mass, approached the altar and were alarmed as they watched the actions of Brother John; and many of them wept in their devotion. At last, after a long interval, when it pleased God, Brother John said in a loud voice: *Corpus Meum*, and at once the likeness of bread vanished from the Host, and Jesus Christ the Blessed appeared incarnate and glorified, revealing the humility and love which moved Him to become incarnate of the Virgin Mary, and which causes Him to come daily into the hands of the priest when he consecrates the Host. And because of this Brother John was even more uplifted in the sweetness of contemplation.

When he had elevated the Host and consecrated the Chalice, Brother John was transported out of himself and his soul was detached from all physical sensation, so that his body fell backwards, and had he not been supported by the Guardian who stood behind him, he would have fallen to the ground. So the friars and the layfolk who were in church, both men and women, ran to him and carried him into the sacristy. And he seemed like a dead man, for his body was cold as a corpse, and the fingers of his hands were so tightly clenched that it was almost impossible to open or move them. And he lay in this state of unconsciousness or rapture until Terce. This was during the summer.

And because I, who was present at this time, greatly desired to learn what God had done within him, I went to him as soon as he had returned to his senses and begged him for the love of God to tell me everything. And because he had great trust in me, he told me everything in due order. And among other things, he told me that while he was meditating on the Body and Blood of Jesus Christ present before him, his heart melted within him like wax before the fire, and his body seemed to be without bones, so that he could hardly raise his arm or hand to make the sign of the Cross over the Host or the Chalice. He also told me that before he was made a priest God revealed to him that he would become unconscious during Mass; but because he had said many Masses without this happening, he thought that the revelation had not been from God. However, about fifty days before the Assumption of our Lady – when the above event actually took place – it had again been revealed to him by God that it would happen during the Feast of the Assumption; but he had not afterwards recalled this revelation.

*

*Here ends the first part of the book of the venerable Saint Francis
and of many of the holy friars who were his companions.
Now follows the second part, which tells of
the holy Stigmata.*

FIVE CONSIDERATIONS ON THE
HOLY STIGMATA OF
SAINT FRANCIS

In this part we shall reverently consider the glorious Stigmata of our blessed Father Saint Francis, which he received from Christ on the summit of the holy Mount La Verna.

Since these Stigmata were five in number, corresponding to the five wounds of Christ, we will treat of them under five considerations.

The first will describe how Saint Francis came to the holy Mount La Verna.

The second will describe his life and conversation with his companions on this holy mountain.

The third will describe his vision of the Seraph and the imprinting of the Stigmata.

The fourth will describe how Saint Francis came down from Mount La Verna after he had received the Stigmata, and returned to Saint Mary of the Angels.

The fifth will describe various visions and divine revelations concerning the glorious Stigmata received by certain friars and other devout persons after the death of Saint Francis.

THE FIRST CONSIDERATION: *How Saint Francis came to the holy Mount La Verna*

As regards this first consideration, it should be known that in the year 1224 Saint Francis, then forty-three years of age, was inspired by God to leave the Vale of Spoleto and go into Romagna with Brother Leo as his companion. As they journeyed they passed by the foot of the castle of Montefeltro, where at the time a grand banquet and assembly was taking place to celebrate the recent knighthood of one of the Counts of Montefeltro. Hearing that this solemn festival was being held, and that many nobles from various districts were assembled there, Saint Francis said to Brother Leo: 'Let us go up here to this festival, for with God's help we may reap a great spiritual harvest.'

Among the other nobles who had come to this assembly was a gentleman of Tuscany whose name was Orlando da Chiusi di Casentino, who, because of the wonderful things he had heard about the holiness of Saint Francis, had a high respect for him and greatly desired to see him and hear him preach.

Reaching the castle, Saint Francis went in and entered the courtyard, where the whole company of gentlemen were gathered, and in fervour of spirit he climbed onto a low wall and began to preach, taking as the theme of his address these words in the vernacular:

> *Tanto è il bene ch'io aspetto*
> *Ch'ogni pene m'è diletto.*

> So great the good I have in sight
> That every pain brings me delight.

And guided by the Holy Spirit, he preached so devoutly and so profoundly on this theme – demonstrating the truth of these words by recounting the various sufferings and martyrdoms of the holy Apostles and Martyrs, the stern penances of holy Confessors, and the many pains and temptations of holy Virgins and other Saints – that everyone remained with their eyes and attention fixed on him, and listened to him as though an angel of God were speaking to them. Among these was the aforesaid Master Orlando, who, touched to the heart by God through the wonderful preaching of Saint Francis, resolved to discuss and take counsel with him about the state of His soul after the sermon. So when the preaching was ended, he drew Saint Francis aside and said: 'Father, I would like to seek your advice on the salvation of my soul.' 'I will be very glad to do so,' answered Saint Francis, 'but this morning go and honour your friends who have invited you to this feast and dine with them; and later, when the dinner is over, we will talk together as long as you wish.' So Orlando went off to the dinner, and afterwards came back to Saint Francis, and gave him a full account of the state of his soul. And in conclusion, Master Orlando said to Saint Francis: 'I possess a mountain in Tuscany called Mount La Verna which is ideal for prayer. It is very lonely and wild, and particularly suitable for any who desire to do penance in a spot remote from men, or to lead a solitary life. If you would like it, I will gladly give it to you and your companions for the salvation of my soul.'

Receiving such a generous offer of the very thing that he so greatly desired, Saint Francis was filled with the greatest joy, and when he had given praise and thanks firstly to God and then to Master Orlando, he said to him: 'Sir, when you have returned to your own home, I will send two of my companions to you, and you can show them this mountain. And if it seems to them a fitting place for prayer and penance, I will immediately accept your kindly offer.'

With this, Saint Francis went away, and when he had completed his travels, he returned to Saint Mary of the Angels. And when the celebrations came to an end, Master Orlando also returned to his castle, which is called Chiusi and stands about a mile from La Verna. When Saint Francis had returned to Saint Mary of the Angels, he sent two of his companions to Master Orlando, who, when they arrived, welcomed them with great joy and kindness. And wishing to show them Mount La Verna, he sent them with about fifty armed men to protect them against wild beasts. And thus escorted, the friars climbed to the top of the mountain and surveyed it thoroughly. And at length they found an area of the mountain well suited to contemplation, part of which consisted of a level plateau. They chose this spot for their dwelling and that of Saint Francis, and, with the help of the armed men who accompanied them, they built some little cells with the branches of trees. So having accepted and taken possession of Mount La Verna and the dwellings on that mountain in the name of God, they departed. And when they had returned to Saint Francis, they told him how they had taken possession of a site on Mount La Verna very suitable for prayer and contemplation.

When Saint Francis heard this news he was filled with joy, and when he had given thanks and praise to God, he said to the friars with a happy face: 'My sons, we are now approaching our fast of Saint Michael the Archangel; I firmly believe it to be God's will that we should observe this fast on Mount La Verna, where God's providence has prepared a place for us, so that by doing penance we may deserve of Christ to consecrate this blessed mountain to the honour and glory of God, and of His glorious Mother the Virgin Mary, and of the holy angels.' After this Saint Francis took with him Brother Masseo da Marignano of Assisi, a man of great wisdom and eloquence, and Brother Angelo Tancredi of Assisi, who was a great gentleman and had been a knight in secular life, and Brother Leo, a man of great simplicity and purity, so that Saint Francis had a great love for him and confided to him almost all his secrets. With these three companions Saint Francis entered into prayer, and when he had ended, he commended himself and his companions to the prayers of the friars remaining behind, and set out with these three friars in the name of Jesus Christ the Crucified to go to Mount La Verna. As Saint Francis was leaving, he called Brother Masseo, one of the companions, and said to him: 'Brother Masseo, you shall be our Guardian and superior on this journey while we are travelling together; and we will observe our good custom either to recite the Office or to keep silence, and we shall not make any plans about what to eat or where to sleep. But when it is time to seek shelter, we will beg a little bread, and stop to rest in whatever place God makes ready for us.' Then the three companions bowed their heads, and making the sign of the holy cross, set out on their way.

On the first evening they reached a house of the friars and lodged there. But on the second evening, owing to bad weather and their own weariness, they could not reach any friary, nor any castle or village; and as night fell and the bad weather continued, they took shelter in a ruined and disused church, and lay down to rest there. And while the companions slept, Saint Francis began to pray; and during the first watch of the night a horde of the fiercest devils came upon him with great clamour and violence as he prayed, and began to assault and torment him. One of them struck him here, another there; one dragged him up, and another down; one threatened him with one thing, another accused him of that. Thus by various means they strove to interrupt his prayer, but did not attain their purpose because God was with him.

So when Saint Francis had resisted these attacks of the devils for a long time, he cried in a loud voice: 'O damned spirits, you can do nothing but what the hand of God allows. I tell you in the name of Almighty God you may do to my body whatever God permits, and I will readily endure it, seeing that I have no greater enemy than my own body. So if you avenge me on my own body, you will do me a great service.' Then the devils seized him with great violence and fury, and began to drag him about the church, and to inflict even greater hurt and distress upon him. Then Saint Francis cried out and said: 'My Lord Jesus Christ, I thank Thee for the great love and charity that Thou showest me, since it is proof of great love when the Lord punishes His servant in full for all his faults in this world, so that he will not be punished

in the next. I am ready to bear gladly every pain and affliction that Thou, O God, seest fit to visit upon me for my
sins.'

Then the devils, confounded and vanquished by his constancy and patience, left him. And Saint Francis, in fervour
of spirit, went out of the church and entered a wood near by.
And there he began to pray, and with supplications, tears,
and beating of the breast sought to find Christ, the Spouse
and Beloved of his soul. Now he called on Him with reverence
as his Lord, now answered to Him as his Judge; now he implored Him as his Father, now conversed with Him as his
friend.

During that night in the wood his companions, who had
woken and come out to listen and watch what he was doing,
saw and heard him calling devoutly and with tears for God's
mercy on sinners. He was also seen and heard by them
lamenting aloud the Passion of Christ, as though he were
watching it with his bodily eyes. During the same night they
saw him at prayer, with his arms outstretched in the form of
a cross, suspended and raised above the ground for a long
time and surrounded by a shining cloud. And so in such holy
exercises he passed the whole night without sleeping.

In the morning the companions realized that Saint Francis
was physically exhausted by his exertions during the night
and by lack of sleep and would hardly be capable of travelling on foot, so they went to a poor peasant in the fields and
begged him for the love of God to lend his donkey for Brother
Francis their father, who was unable to travel on foot. Hearing them mention Brother Francis, he asked them: 'Are you
some of the friars of that Brother Francis of Assisi of whom
so much good is spoken?' The friars replied that they were,
and that it was for Saint Francis himself that they were seeking
the donkey. Then the good fellow made ready the donkey
with great devotion and care, and led him to Saint Francis.
And with great respect he helped him to mount and continue

on his way. And he went with them, walking behind his donkey.

When they had gone some distance the peasant said to Saint Francis: 'Tell me, are you Brother Francis of Assisi?' Saint Francis answered, 'Yes.' 'In that case,' said the man, 'try to be as good as everyone imagines you to be, for the people have great trust in you. So I warn you, don't be any different from what people expect.' When Saint Francis heard these words he was not angry at being warned by a peasant, nor did he say to himself, 'What creature is this who gives me advice?', as many proud men who wear the cowl in these days would say. But he immediately dismounted from the donkey and knelt on the ground before the man; and he kissed his feet, and thanked him humbly for having deigned to counsel him with such charity. Then the peasant and the companions of Saint Francis raised him from the ground with great devotion, and lifting him on to the donkey again, they continued their journey.

And when they had climbed about half-way up the mountain, the peasant began to suffer from a raging thirst, for the heat was great and the ascent exhausting. So he called out behind Saint Francis: 'Alas, I am dying of thirst! If I don't find something to drink I shall faint this instant.' So Saint Francis dismounted from the donkey and knelt down to pray; and he remained kneeling with his hands upraised to heaven until he knew by revelation that God had granted his request. Then he said to the peasant: 'Run at once to that rock, and there you will find living water which Christ in His mercy has caused to issue from the rock in this very hour.' The man ran to the spot that Saint Francis pointed out to him, and found a beautiful spring drawn from the hard rock by the virtue of Saint Francis's prayer, and he drank deeply and was comforted. And it was abundantly clear that this spring was miraculously produced by God at the prayer of Saint Francis, for neither before nor since was a spring of water ever seen at that spot, nor was there any running water for a considerable distance around. After this, Saint Francis with his companions and the peasant gave thanks to God for the miracle He had shown them, and continued on their way.

As they approached the foot of the rocks around La Verna itself, Saint Francis wished to rest awhile beneath an oak tree which stood by the track, and remains there today. And as he rested there, Saint Francis began to gaze around the place and the surrounding countryside. And while he was doing this there came a great flock of birds of many kinds, which showed the greatest joy and pleasure by singing and flapping their wings. And as they gathered around Saint Francis some alighted on his head, some on his shoulders, some on his arms, some on his knees, and around his feet. When his companions and the peasant saw this they were amazed, and in great exaltation of spirit Saint Francis said to them: 'My dearest brothers, I believe it to be the pleasure of our Lord Jesus Christ that we should dwell on this lonely mountain, because our sisters and brothers the birds show such joy at our coming.' And with these words he rose and they travelled on, and arrived at length at the place which his companions had chosen earlier.

To the praise of God. Amen.

And this is all that concerns our first consideration, how Saint Francis came to Mount La Verna.

THE SECOND CONSIDERATION: *On the sayings and life of Saint Francis on Mount La Verna*

THE second consideration concerns the converse of Saint Francis with his companions on this holy mountain. As for this, it should be known that when Master Orlando heard that Saint Francis had gone up to live on Mount La Verna with three companions, he was very pleased, and on the following day he set out from his castle with a large following and went to visit him, bringing bread and other necessities of life for him and his companions. On reaching the summit he found them engaged in prayer, and coming towards them, he gave them greeting. Then Saint Francis rose and welcomed Master Orlando and his people with great love and joy, and afterwards they talked together. And when they had conversed for a while, and Saint Francis had thanked him for the holy mountain he had given them and for his visit, he requested Master Orlando to have a rough cell made for him at the foot of a beautiful beech tree that stood about a stone's throw from the dwelling of the friars, since this seemed to him a secluded place and very suitable for prayer. Master Orlando immediately had this done, and later, as evening was approaching and it was time to leave, Saint Francis addressed them briefly before they went away. And when he had preached and given them his blessing, Master Orlando made ready to leave, and calling Saint Francis and his companions apart, he said to them: 'My dearest brothers, while you are on this wild mountain I do not wish you to suffer any bodily need, which would make you less able to devote yourself to spiritual things. So I tell you this once for all; I want you to send freely to my house for anything you need, and if you don't do this, I shall be very hurt.' And with these words, he left with his company and returned to the castle.

Then Saint Francis made his companions sit down, and instructed them on the way of life which they and any others who might wish to live the life of religion in hermitages should lead. Among other things, he imposed on them in particular the observance of holy poverty, saying: 'Do not avail yourselves overmuch of Master Orlando's generous offer lest in any way you offend our mistress, Lady Poverty. You can be certain that the more we despise poverty, the more will the world despise us, and the greater want we shall endure;

but if we embrace holy poverty as closely as we can, the world will certainly follow us and provide abundantly for us. God has called us to this life of holy Religion for the salvation of the world, and has made a pact between us and the world, that we set the world a good example and that the world provides for our needs. So let us persevere in holy poverty, for it is the way of perfection, and the token and pledge of eternal riches.'

After many eloquent and devout words and counsel on such matters, he ended: 'This is the way of life which I impose on myself and on you; and because I realize that my death is drawing near, I propose to remain in retirement and be alone with God, and to weep over my sins before Him. At whatever times he thinks fit, Brother Leo will bring me a little bread and a little water. And on no account allow any layfolk to visit me, but speak to them on my behalf.'

So saying, he gave them his blessing and retired to the cell under the beech tree. And the companions remained in their own dwelling, firmly resolved to carry out Saint Francis's orders. A few days later, while Saint Francis was standing by his cell gazing at the outline of the mountain and wondering at the great fissures and cracks in its mighty rocks, he entered into prayer, and it was then revealed to him that these amazing fissures had been caused miraculously at the hour of Christ's Passion, when, according to the Evangelist, the rocks were rent apart. And God willed that this should appear in an especial way on Mount La Verna, to show that on this mountain the Passion of Christ Jesus was to be renewed in the soul of Saint Francis by love and compassion, and in his body by the impression of the Stigmata.

When Saint Francis had received this revelation, he at once entered into recollection himself and prepared to comprehend the mystery that was to be revealed. And thenceforward, through constant prayer, Saint Francis began to experience more frequently the sweetness of divine contemplation, by which he was so rapt in God that he was seen by his companions raised bodily from the ground and transported out of himself.

During these contemplative ecstasies not only were present and future events revealed to him by God, but even the hidden thoughts and desires of the friars, as Brother Leo his companion proved by personal experience at that time. For Brother Leo was undergoing a severe temptation by the devil – not of a carnal, but of a spiritual nature – when there came upon him a great desire to possess some holy words written by the hand of Saint Francis himself; and he thought that if he could obtain this, the temptation would leave him, either completely or partially. But although he had this desire, yet through shame and reverence he did not have the courage to tell Saint Francis. But this unspoken desire of Brother Leo was revealed to him by the Holy Spirit. So Saint Francis called Brother Leo to him, and made him bring ink, pen, and parchment, and with his own hand wrote a praise of Christ, just as Brother Leo had desired; and at the same time he made the sign *Tau*,* and gave it to him, saying: 'Take this paper, dearest brother, and keep it carefully till your death. May God bless you, and preserve you in every temptation. Do not be dismayed because you have temptations, for on this account I regard you even more as the servant of God; and the more severely you are troubled by temptations, the greater the love I bear you. I tell you in all truth, that no one may regard himself as a perfect friend of God until he has endured many temptations and troubles.'

Brother Leo received this writing with the greatest devotion and faith, and all temptation immediately left him. And on his return to the companions' dwelling, he told them most joyfully how great a grace God had given him when he received this writing from the hand of Saint Francis. And

---

* Saint Francis's blessing of Brother Leo. This blessing, the original of which is preserved at Assisi, is given in full in Appendix 5.

putting it away and preserving it carefully, the friars later worked many miracles by means of it.

From that hour onward Brother Leo, with great purity and good intention, began to observe and closely consider the life of Saint Francis; and because of his purity he was on many occasions allowed to see Saint Francis rapt in God and raised from the ground, sometimes to a height of four feet, sometimes five, and some times level with the top of the beech tree. And sometimes he saw him raised so high in the air and surrounded by so brilliant a splendour that he could hardly see him. And what did this simple friar do when Saint Francis was raised only a short distance from the ground, so that he could touch him? He would approach softly and embrace his feet, kissing them with tears, and saying: 'God, have mercy on me a sinner, and through the merits of this holy man grant me to find grace with Thee.' And on one such occasion, while he was standing thus below Saint Francis's feet as he was raised so far above the earth that he could not touch him, he saw a scroll, written in letters of gold, descend from heaven and rest on the head of Saint Francis; and on this scroll were written these words: 'Here is the grace of God.' And when he had read it, he saw it return to heaven.

By this gift of God's grace within him, Saint Francis was not only caught up to God in ecstatic contemplation, but was also comforted by the visits of angels. One day, while Saint Francis was meditating on his death and of the state of his Order after his death, he said: 'Lord God, after my death what will become of Thy poor little family, which in Thy goodness Thou has entrusted to me, a sinner? Who will comfort it? Who will correct it? Who will pray to Thee for it?' And while he was praying on these things, an angel sent by God appeared to him and comforted him, saying: 'I promise you, in the name of God, that the profession of your Order shall not fail until the Day of Judgement; and no one, however great a sinner, shall fail to find mercy with God if he loves the Order with all his heart. And none who maliciously persecutes your Order will enjoy long life. Furthermore, no wicked member of your Order will be able to remain in it for long unless he amends his life. Do not be grieved, therefore, if you see in the Order a certain number of friars who are not good, and who do not keep the Rule as they should; and do not think that the Order will decline on their account, for there will always be a great number who will follow Christ's gospel way of life perfectly, and observe the Rule in its purity. Immediately after the death of the body, these shall enter eternal life without passing through Purgatory; others will observe the Rule, but not perfectly, and these shall pass through Purgatory before they enter Paradise, but God will delegate to you the length of their purgation. But as for those who do not observe the Rule at all, God bids you have no concern for them, for God Himself has no concern for them.' With these words the angel departed, and Saint Francis remained completely comforted and consoled.

As the Feast of the Assumption of our Lady drew near, Saint Francis sought a more lonely and remote place where he could keep in greater solitude the Fast of Saint Michael, which begins on this Feast of the Assumption. So he called Brother Leo and said to him: 'Go and stand at the door of the oratory of the friars' dwelling, and when I call you come back to me.' So Brother Leo went and stood at the door, and Saint Francis withdrew to a distance and called loudly. Hearing him call, Brother Leo came back to him, and Saint Francis said: 'My son, let us look for another place more remote, where you cannot hear me when I call.' And as they searched, they saw on the southern slope of the mountain a remote spot very well suited to their purpose, but they could not reach it because an awful and terrifying rocky precipice lay in front of it. So with great efforts they laid a log across the chasm to form a bridge, and crossed over.

Then Saint Francis sent for the other friars, and told them

how he intended to keep the Fast of Saint Michael in this solitary place; and he asked them to build him a little cell there, where no cry of his could be heard by them. And when the cell had been built, Saint Francis said to them: 'Now return to your own dwelling and leave me alone, for with God's help I intend to keep this fast without being disturbed or distracted in mind; so let none of you come to me. But you only, Brother Leo, come to me once a day with a little bread and water, and again during the night at the hour of Matins. Then come in silence, and when you reach the end of the bridge, you are to say: "*Domine, labia mea aperies*" ("Lord, open Thou my lips"), and if I answer, cross over and come to the cell, and we will say Matins together; but if I do not answer you, then go away at once.' And Saint Francis said this because he was at times so rapt in God that he was not conscious of anything through his bodily senses. And with these instructions, Saint Francis gave them his blessing, and they returned to their own dwelling.

When the Feast of the Assumption arrived, Saint Francis began to keep the fast with the strictest abstinence and austerity, mortifying his body and fortifying his soul by fervent prayer, vigil, and discipline; and by these means he steadily advanced from grace to grace, preparing his soul to receive the divine mysteries and splendours, and his body to withstand the savage attacks of devils, with whom he often engaged in bodily conflict. One day during this fast Saint Francis came out of his cell in fervour of spirit, and went a short distance to pray in the hollow of an overhanging crag, in front of which a terrible and frightening precipice fell away from a dizzy height to the earth below. Here the devil suddenly came at him in horrible form with a great tempest and uproar, and struck him in order to hurl him down. Having no means of escape and unable to endure the hideous appearance of the devil, Saint Francis turned swiftly and pressed his face and entire body against the rock; and commending himself to

God, he groped with his hands for something to which he could cling. But God, who never allows His servants to be tried beyond their strength, miraculously caused the rock against which he was pressing suddenly to yield itself into the shape of his body and receive him into itself as though he had placed his hands and feet into melted wax, so that the form of his face and hands remained imprinted on this rock; and by God's help he escaped from the devil.

However, what the devil was then unable to do to Saint Francis – that is, to hurl him down the precipice – he did a long time after the death of Saint Francis to a beloved and devout friar who, out of devotion to Saint Francis and the miracle that had happened there, was fixing some planks of wood there so that he could visit the spot without danger. For one day the devil pushed him when he was carrying on his head a large plank, which he was about to place in position, and caused him to fall with the plank still on his head. But God, who had rescued and preserved Saint Francis from falling, by His merits preserved and rescued His devout friar from the dangers of the fall. For as he fell, this friar in a loud voice commended himself most devoutly to God and Saint Francis, who immediately appeared and caught him, setting him down on the rocks without shock or hurt.

Having heard him cry out as he fell, the other friars imagined him dead and dashed to pieces by his fall on the jagged rocks. So with great grief and lamentation they took a litter and went round the other side of the mountain to recover his body and bury it. And when they had descended the mountain, the friar who had fallen met them, carrying the log on his head and singing *Te Deum Laudamus* in a loud voice. The friars were completely dumbfounded, so the friar gave them a full account of his fall, and told them how Saint Francis had preserved him from all danger. Then all the friars went with him to the spot, singing the *Te Deum*, and praising and thanking God and Saint Francis for the miracle He had performed for His friar. But let us now return to the doings of Saint Francis, which we had begun to relate.

As we have already described, while Saint Francis was keeping the fast, he endured many assaults from the devil; nevertheless, he received many consolations and revelations from God, not only through visits from angels but from wild birds as well. For during the whole period of the fast, a falcon which had built her nest close to his cell used to rouse him each night before Matins by her cry and by beating her wings against the cell, and she would not go away until he rose to say Matins. And whenever Saint Francis was more weary than usual, or weak or ill, this falcon, like a wise and compassionate person, used to utter her cry a little later. Saint Francis took great delight in this holy time-keeper, for the falcon's solicitude banished all sloth and summoned him to prayer, and furthermore the bird often used to spend the day with him.

Lastly, as regards this second consideration, Saint Francis became weakened in body by his severe fasting and his conflicts with devils, and wished to sustain the body by the spiritual nourishment of his soul. And he began to meditate on the boundless glory and happiness of the blessed spirits in life everlasting, and prayed God to grant him the favour to experience a little of that joy. And while he was thinking on this matter, an angel suddenly appeared to him in great splendour, holding a viol in his left hand and a bow in his right. And as Saint Francis was gazing in wonder at the appearance of this angel, he drew the bow once across the viol, and immediately the soul of Saint Francis was entranced by a melody of such infinite sweetness that he was robbed of all physical sensation. Indeed, as he afterwards told his companions, he felt that, had the angel drawn his bow back across the strings, his soul would assuredly have parted from his body, so unbearable was the sweetness. And this is all that concerns the second consideration.

CONCERNING the third consideration, that is, of the vision of the Seraph and the imprinting of the Stigmata: one night in September just before the Feast of the Holy Cross,* Brother Leo went at the usual hour to say Matins with Saint Francis. And when he called *Domine, labia mea aperies* from the end of the bridge as usual, Saint Francis did not answer. Brother Leo did not turn back as Saint Francis had directed him, but with a good and holy intention he crossed the bridge and softly entered his cell. Not finding him there, he thought that he might have gone to some place in the wood to pray; so he came out, and by the light of the moon, went quietly searching for him in the wood. At length he heard Saint Francis's voice, and as he came nearer saw him kneeling with his face and hands upraised to heaven, exclaiming with great fervour of spirit: 'Who art Thou, sweetest Lord God? And what am I, Thy worthless servant?' And he continued to repeat these words, saying nothing else.

Full of wonder, Brother Leo raised his eyes and saw a lovely and radiant torch of fire descend from heaven and come to rest over the head of Saint Francis. And out of this flame he heard a voice speaking to Saint Francis. But Brother Leo could not understand the words. When he saw this, he felt himself unworthy to remain so near that holy place where such a wonderful thing was taking place; and fearing to offend Saint Francis by interrupting this spiritual experience if he were noticed, Brother Leo stole quietly away, and remained at a distance, waiting to see the end. Watching closely, he saw Saint Francis extend his hands towards the flame three times, and at length, after a long interval, he saw the flame return to heaven.

After this Brother Leo moved away, content and happy at

* 14 September.

the vision, and turned back towards his cell. But as he was walking confidently away, Saint Francis heard him by the rustle of the leaves under his feet, and told him to halt and not to move. Then Brother Leo obediently halted and waited with such fear that, as he afterwards told his companions, at that moment he would have rather had the earth swallow him up than wait for Saint Francis, because he feared that he would be displeased with him. For he always took the greatest care not to offend his Father, lest through any fault of his Saint Francis should deny him his company.

When Saint Francis came up to him, he asked: 'Who are you?'

Trembling all over, Brother Leo replied: 'I am Leo, my Father.'

And Saint Francis said to him: 'Why have you come here, Brother Little Sheep? Haven't I told you not to come watching me? Tell me, under holy obedience, have you heard or seen anything?'

Brother Leo answered: 'Father, I heard you say and repeat many times, "Who art Thou, sweetest God? And who am I, a wretched worm, Thy worthless servant?" ' Then, kneeling down before Saint Francis, Brother Leo accused himself of the sin of disobedience that he had committed by disobeying his command, and asked pardon with many tears. And afterwards he earnestly begged Saint Francis to explain these words which he had not understood.

Then Saint Francis, realizing that God had allowed the humble Brother Leo to see certain things because of his simplicity and purity, was pleased to reveal and explain to him what he had asked. And he said to him: 'Brother Little Sheep of Jesus Christ, understand that when I said those words that you heard, two lights were shown me within my soul; one was the knowledge and understanding of the Creator, and the other was the knowledge of myself. When I said: "Who art Thou, my sweetest God?", I was in the light of contemplation, in which I saw the infinite depths of the goodness, wisdom, and power of God. And when I said: "What am I? etc.", I was in the light of contemplation in which I saw the profound sorrow of my own wretchedness and misery. That is why I said: "Who art Thou, Lord of infinite goodness, wisdom and power, who deignest to visit me, who am a vile worm?" God was in that flame which you saw, and spoke to me in that form as He spoke in old times to Moses. And among other things that He said to me, He asked me to offer three gifts. "I am wholly Thine," I answered: "Thou knowest that I possess nothing but the habit, the cord, and the under-garment, and even these three things are Thine. What can I offer to Thy Majesty?" Then God said: "Search within your breast, and offer Me what you find there." I searched and found a ball of gold, and this I offered to God. I did this three times, as God commanded me; and then I knelt three times, and blessed and thanked God, who had given me something to offer. And forthwith it was given me to understand that these three offerings represented holy Obedience, highest Poverty, and resplendent Charity, which things by His grace God had granted me to observe so perfectly that my conscience in no way reproaches me. And as you saw me put my hand into my breast and offer God these three virtues, represented by the three golden balls which God had placed within my breast, so has God placed within my soul this virtue, that I should praise and glorify Him for all the blessings and graces which, in His holy goodness, He has granted me. It was these words that you heard when you saw me raise my hands three times. But beware, Brother Little Sheep, that you do not go watching me; return to your cell with God's blessing, and take great care of me, for in a few days God will perform great and marvellous things on this mountain, at which the whole world will wonder. For He will do some new thing, the like of which He has never done to any creature in this world.'

Having said this, Saint Francis had the Book of the Gospels brought to him, for God had put it into his soul that, by opening the Book of the Gospels three times, it would be shown him what it would please God to do to him. And when the book had been brought, Saint Francis knelt in prayer; and when his prayer was ended, he had the Book opened three times by the hand of Brother Leo in the name of the Holy Trinity. And it pleased divine providence that on each occasion the Passion of Christ came to view. In this way he was given to understand that, as he had followed Christ in the actions of his life, so he was also to follow and be conformed to Him in the pains and sorrows of His Passion before departing this life. And thenceforward Saint Francis began to experience and savour in ever-increasing measure the sweetness of divine contemplation and of divine visitations. And in one of these he received an immediate preparation for the impression of the Stigmata, which took this form.

The day before the Feast of the Holy Cross in September, while Saint Francis was at prayer alone in his cell, an angel of God appeared to him and spoke to him in God's name: 'I have come to comfort and counsel you to prepare and dispose yourself humbly and with all patience to accept the thing that God wills to perform in you.'

'I am ready to endure patiently everything that my Lord desires to do with me,' replied Saint Francis. And when he had said this, the angel departed.

The next day, the Feast of the Holy Cross, before dawn Saint Francis was kneeling in prayer at the entrance to his cell, and turning his face towards the east, he uttered this prayer: 'My Lord Jesus Christ, I pray Thee grant me two favours before I die: the first, that during my lifetime I may feel in my own body, so far as is possible, the anguish which Thou, sweet Jesus, didst feel in the hour of Thy most bitter Passion; the second, that I may feel in my heart, so far as is possible, the boundless love wherewith Thou, the Son of

God, wert moved, and willed to bear such agony for us sinners.' And as he continued a long while in this prayer, he knew that God would grant it, and that, so far as is possible to a mere creature, he would be permitted to experience these things as he had asked.

When Saint Francis had received this assurance, he began to contemplate the Passion of Christ and His boundless love with great devotion, and his fervour grew so strong within him that he became wholly transformed into Jesus through love and compassion. And on this same morning, while he was thus inflamed by this contemplation, he saw a Seraph with six shining, fiery wings descend from heaven. This Seraph drew near to Saint Francis in swift flight, so that he could see him clearly and recognize that he had the form of a man crucified. His wings were disposed in such a way that two stretched up above his head, two were spread in flight, and the other two covered his whole body. As Saint Francis gazed on him he was filled with great fear, and at the same time with great joy, sorrow, and wonder. He felt great joy at the gracious face of Christ, who appeared to him so familiarly and looked on him so kindly; but seeing Him nailed to the Cross, he felt infinite sorrow and compassion. Then he fell to wondering at this stupendous and unprecedented vision, knowing full well that the weakness of the Passion did not accord with the immortality of the Seraphic spirit. And while he was wondering, it was revealed to him by the Seraph that the vision had been shown to him in this form by divine providence, because God willed that he should be wholly transformed into the express likeness of Christ Crucified, not by the martyrdom of his body, but by the kindling of his soul.

During this wondrous vision the whole mountain of La Verna appeared glowing with brilliant flame, which lit up all the mountain and the valleys around it as though the sun had risen over the earth. Because of this shepherds watching their flocks in the countryside, seeing the mountain aflame and enveloped by so brilliant a light, were greatly alarmed, and later told the friars that this flame remained over the mountain of La Verna for an hour or more. In the same way, some mule-drivers travelling into Romagna were roused by the brightness of this light, which shone through the windows of the country inns, and got up, thinking that the sun had risen. They saddled and loaded their beasts, and as they set out on the road, they saw this light die away and the real sun rise.

During this seraphic vision Christ appeared to Saint Francis and revealed a number of high and secret things which He would never disclose to anyone during His lifetime, but after His death he revealed them as will be told later. And these were His words: 'Do you know,' said Christ, 'what I have done to you? I have given you the Stigmata, which are the marks of My Passion, so that you may be My Standard-Bearer. And as I descended into Limbo on the day of My death, and delivered all the souls there by the merits of My Stigmata, so do I grant you each year on the anniversary of your death to visit Purgatory, and by the virtue of your Stigmata you shall release all the souls whom you shall find there belonging to your three Orders – namely Friars Minor, Sisters, and Penitents – as well as others who have had great devotion to you, and you shall lead them to the glory of Paradise. In this way you shall be conformed to Me in My death as you have been during your life.'

Then after a long period of secret converse this marvellous vision faded, leaving in the heart of Saint Francis a glowing flame of divine love, and in his body a wonderful image and imprint of the Passion of Christ. For in the hands and feet of Saint Francis forthwith began to appear the marks of the nails in the same manner as he had seen them in the body of Jesus Crucified, who had appeared to him in the form of a Seraph. So his hands and feet appeared to have been pierced through the centre by nails, the heads of which were in the palms of his hands and the soles of his feet, standing out from the flesh; and their points issued from the backs of the hands and feet, so that they seemed to have been bent back and clinched in such a fashion that a finger could easily have been thrust through the bend outside the flesh as though through a ring; and the heads of the nails were round and black. Similarly in his right side appeared an unhealed lance wound, red and bleeding, from which blood often flowed from the holy heart of Saint Francis, staining his habit and under-garment.

Before his companions knew about these things from him, they nevertheless noticed that he did not uncover his hands or feet, and that he could not set his feet to the ground. And finding that his habit and under-garment were stained with blood when they washed them, they knew for certain that he bore the image and likeness of Christ Crucified imprinted on his hands and feet, as well as in his side. And although he did his best to cover and conceal these glorious Stigmata thus clearly imprinted on his body, he realized that he could hardly hide them from his intimate companions. But fearing to reveal the secrets of God, he was in great perplexity whether or not he ought to reveal the seraphic vision and the impression of the Stigmata. At length, under pressure from his conscience, he called some of his most intimate friars to him, and set forth his doubts in general terms without revealing the facts, asking their counsel as to what he should do. Among these friars was one of great holiness, whose name was Brother Illuminato. Understanding that Saint Francis must have seen something marvellous, he answered: 'Brother Francis remember that God has several times revealed His secrets to you, not for your own benefit alone, but for that of others as well. You may well deserve reproof if you conceal something that God has revealed to you for the benefit of others.' Then Saint Francis, moved by these words, related all the circumstances and nature of the vision with the greatest awe, adding that Christ, who had appeared to him, had told him certain things which he could not disclose during his lifetime. And although these most holy wounds, inasmuch as they had been imprinted by Christ, filled his heart with the greatest joy, yet in his flesh and bodily senses they gave him intolerable pain. So, constrained by necessity, he chose Brother Leo, the most simple and pure of the friars, and told him everything. And he allowed him to touch and bind these holy wounds with bandages, in order to ease his pain and staunch the blood that flowed from them. In times of sickness he permitted him to change these bandages frequently, sometimes daily, except between Thursday evening and Saturday morning, for during that period he was not willing that the pain of Christ's Passion, which he endured in his own body, should be eased by any human remedy or medicine; for during that time our Lord and Saviour had been crucified, died, and buried for our sakes. Once, when Brother Leo was changing the bandages from the wound in his side, Saint Francis, because of the pain he felt at the removal of the bloodstained dressings, rested his hand on Brother Leo's breast; and at the touch of these holy hands Brother Leo felt such sweetness of devotion in his heart that he nearly fell fainting to the ground.

Lastly, as concerns this third consideration, having ended the Fast of Saint Michael the Archangel, Saint Francis was moved by God to make ready to return to Saint Mary of the Angels. So he called Brother Masseo and Brother Angelo to him, and when he had spoken with them a long while and given them sacred instructions, he entrusted the holy mountain to their care with all the earnestness at his command, telling them that it was necessary for him to return to Saint Mary of the Angels with Brother Leo. This done, he took leave of them, and blessed them in the name of Jesus Crucified; and in response to their request he extended his most holy hands, adorned by the glorious Stigmata, so that they could see, touch, and kiss them. And leaving them thus comforted, he left them and descended the holy mountain.

End of the Third Consideration.

THE FOURTH CONSIDERATION: *The miracles which occurred after the Holy Stigmata*

Regarding this fourth consideration, let it be known that when the true love of Christ had perfectly transformed Saint Francis into the true likeness of God and of Christ Crucified, and when he had ended the forty days' fast in honour of Saint Michael on the summit of Mount La Verna, Saint Francis came down from the mountain after the Feast of Saint Michael with Brother Leo and a devout peasant, on whose ass he rode; for because of the nails in his feet he could hardly set foot to the ground. When he had come down from the mountain the people of the countryside heard that he was approaching, and hastened to meet him, for the report of his holiness had been spread far and wide throughout the land, and the shepherds had told how they had seen the whole mountain wrapped in flame, and that this must be the sign of some great miracle which God had wrought in Saint Francis. So men and women, great and small, all came with great devotion, wishing to touch and kiss his hands. And Saint Francis, unable to disregard the people's devotion, allowed them to kiss the tips of his fingers, although his palms had been bandaged, and the better to hide the Stigmata, he also covered them with his sleeves. But although he did his best to conceal the mystery of the holy Stigmata, in order to avoid all occasion of worldly glory, it pleased God to display many miracles to His Own glory by the virtue of these Stigmata, especially during the Saint's journey from La Verna to Saint Mary of the Angels. And numerous other miracles took place in different parts of the world, both during his life and after his glorious death, in order that the secret and wondrous virtue of the Stigmata, and the love and mercy of Christ shown him in so marvellous a manner, might be displayed to the world by clear and unmistakable miracles, of which we will relate a few.

Once, as Saint Francis was approaching a village on the boundaries of the district of Arezzo, a woman came to him weeping bitterly, carrying her little son in her arms. The child was eight years old, and for four years had been afflicted with dropsy, and his stomach was so distended that when he stood upright he could not see his feet. And setting down the child before him, the woman implored Saint Francis to pray to God for him. Saint Francis first entered into prayer, and when his prayer was ended, he laid his holy hands on the child's stomach; and immediately the swelling vanished, and he was perfectly healed. Then Saint Francis restored him to his mother, who received him with great joy and led him home thanking God and His saint. And she gladly showed her little boy, now restored to health, to everyone who lived in the district and visited her home to see him.

The same day Saint Francis passed through Borgo San Sepolcro, and before he reached the castle the people of the castle and the town came out to meet him, and many of them walked in front of him with olive branches in their hands, shouting: 'Here comes the Saint! Here comes the Saint!' And a great crowd gathered round him, because of the devotion of the people and their desire to touch him. But Saint Francis travelled onward with his mind upraised to God and rapt in contemplation, passing through the people as though insensible, although they touched, clasped, and pulled at him. He was not aware of anything that was done or said around him, nor did he realize that he was passing through that town and district. So when he had passed through the town, and the crowd had dispersed to their homes, he came to a leper-house a good mile beyond; and returning to himself like one coming back from another world, this heavenly contemplative asked his companion: 'When shall we be nearing Borgo?' For his soul, rooted and transported in contemplation of heavenly things, had been completely unconscious of all worldly things, and had not noticed any change of place, passing of time, or people he met. And this was often the case, as his companions clearly proved by experience.

That evening Saint Francis reached the friary at Monte Casale, where there lived a friar so cruelly sick and horribly tormented by his disease that he seemed to be tormented by the devil rather than by a natural malady. For sometimes he used to hurl himself to the ground, trembling violently and foaming at the mouth; sometimes he contracted all his limbs, sometimes he stretched them out; sometimes he would writhe about, or twist his heels about his neck, or leap into the air and immediately fall on his back. While Saint Francis was at table he heard about the remarkable and incurable malady of this brother from the other friars, and was filled with compassion. And he took a piece of bread that he was eating, and making the sign of the Cross upon it with his holy hands marked by the Stigmata, he sent it to the sick brother. And as soon as the sick man had eaten it, he was completely cured, and never again suffered from this malady.

The following morning Saint Francis sent two of the friars of that house to go and live on La Verna, and with them he sent back the peasant who had walked behind the ass he had lent them, wishing him to return home in their company. The brothers left with the peasant, and coming to the neighbourhood of Arezzo, they were seen a long way off by some country folk, who were filled with great joy, thinking that it was Saint Francis, who had passed through two days earlier. For there was a woman in the place about to give birth, and she had already been in labour three days and been unable to bring forth, so that she was at death's door; and they thought that if Saint Francis were to lay his holy hands on her, she would recover. But when the friars drew nearer, and they saw that it was not Saint Francis, they were very disappointed. But although the Saint was not present in person, his power was not lacking because their faith was not lacking. Marvellous to tell, the woman was dying, and the signs of death were already apparent. The people asked the friars whether they had anything that had been touched by the holy hands of Saint Francis. The friars thought and searched carefully, and found nothing that he had touched except the halter of the ass on whose back he had ridden. Taking this halter with great reverence and devotion, they laid it on the body of the pregnant woman, devoutly calling on the name of Saint Francis, and commending her to him with firm faith. And as soon as the halter had been laid on the woman she was delivered from all danger, and joyfully gave birth with ease and safety.

When Saint Francis had spent several days in that friary,* he left and came to Città di Castello. Here many of the townsfolk brought to him a woman who had long been possessed by a devil, and humbly begged him to set her free, for she disturbed the whole neighbourhood with her dismal howling, harsh shrieks, and dog-like barks. When Saint Francis had prayed to God and made the sign of the Cross over her, he commanded the devil to come out of her; and immediately he came out, leaving her sound in body and mind. And when this miracle was made known among the people, another woman with great faith brought him her little boy who was gravely ill with a severe wound, and she earnestly implored him to make the sign of the cross over him with his hand. Granting her request, Saint Francis took the child, and, removing the bandage from the wound, blessed him, making the sign of the most holy Cross over the wound three times;

* Monte Casale.

then he replaced the bandages with his own hands, and restored him to his mother. And because it was evening, she at once put him to bed to sleep. In the morning when she went to take the child from his bed, she found the bandages undone; and as she looked, she found him completely healed, as though he had never received any hurt; but over the place where the wound had been the flesh had grown together in the form of a red rose. And this was evidence of the miracle rather than the scar of the wound, for this rose remained all the days of his life, and often moved him to a special devotion to Saint Francis who had healed him.

At the earnest request of the townsfolk Saint Francis remained in this city for a month, during which time he performed many other miracles; then he left to go to Saint Mary of the Angels with Brother Leo, together with a good man who lent him an ass on which to ride. But because of bad roads and intense cold, they were unable to reach any house where they could lodge although they travelled all day, so under the compulsion of darkness and bad weather, they took shelter in the hollow of an overhanging crag to avoid the snow and oncoming night. And as they lay there in discomfort and poorly sheltered, the good fellow who owned the ass could not sleep because of the cold. And since there was no means of making a fire, he began to grumble quietly to himself and to groan, complaining against Saint Francis who had brought him to such a spot. When Saint Francis noticed this he had compassion on him; and in fervour of spirit he reached out his hand and touched him. Wonderful to tell, as soon as he touched him with his hand, pierced by the fire of the Seraph, all the cold vanished, and such warmth flowed into him that he seemed to be near a glowing furnace; so, comforted in mind and body, he fell asleep, and that night he slept until dawn among the rocks and snow more soundly than he had ever slept in his own bed.

Next day they continued their journey and came to Saint

Mary of the Angels. And as they drew near, Brother Leo raised his eyes and looked towards Saint Mary of the Angels; and he saw a cross of fairest gold, upon which was the form of the Crucified, going before Saint Francis. And this cross went before the face of Saint Francis, and conformed to his movements; when he stopped, it stopped, and when he went on, it went on. And this Cross shone with such splendour that not only the face of Saint Francis but all the road around shone with glory. When Saint Francis and Brother Leo arrived at the house, they were welcomed by the friars with the greatest joy and affection, and thenceforward until his death Saint Francis spent most of his time at the friary of Saint Mary. And although in his profound humility he concealed the gifts and graces of God as well as he could, and called himself the greatest of sinners, the fame of his holiness and his miracles continued to spread more and more widely throughout the world.

Brother Leo was once marvelling about this, and in his simplicity thought to himself: 'This man calls himself the greatest of sinners in public; he is great in the Order and highly exalted by God. Nonetheless, in private he has confessed to carnal sin: can he be a virgin?' And he began to evince a strong desire to know the truth, but did not presume to ask Saint Francis. So he had recourse to God, and earnestly besought Him to confirm what he desired to know. And through his many prayers he deserved to be heard, and was assured by means of a vision that Saint Francis was indeed a virgin in body. For in this vision he saw Saint Francis standing in a high and lofty place, which no one else could approach or attain; and it was revealed to him that this place, so high and exalted, represented the nobility of virginal purity in Saint Francis, so fitting for his body which was to be adorned with the sacred wounds of Christ.

Saint Francis, recognizing that because of the Stigmata his bodily strength was gradually failing, and that he could no

longer direct the affairs of the Order, summoned the General
Chapter. And when all the friars were assembled in Chapter,
he humbly excused himself to them for the frailty which
made him unable to administer the affairs of the Order in
such a way as to fulfil the office of General; he explained,
however, that he could not resign his office or appoint a suc-
cessor without the express permission of the Pope. But he
nominated Peter Cattani as his Vicar, entrusting the Order to
his care and that of the Ministers of the Provinces with all the
affection in his power. When Saint Francis had done this he
was comforted in spirit, and raising his eyes and hands to
heaven, he said: 'To Thee, my Lord God, I commend Thy
family, which Thou has entrusted to me until this hour;
and now, my sweetest Lord, because of my infirmities, which
Thou knowest, I am no longer able to sustain this charge. I
also entrust it to the Ministers Provincial; let them render
account for it on the Day of Judgement if any friar shall
perish through their neglect, or bad example, or by excessive
correction.' And it pleased God that by these words all the
friars in Chapter understood that, when he excused himself
on account of weakness, he was referring to the Stigmata;
and all wept because of their devotion to him. And thenceforward he left all the affairs and administration of the Order
to his Vicar and to the Ministers Provincial, and said: 'Now
that I have surrendered the responsibilities of the Order because of my weakness, I have now no duties save to pray to
God for our Order, and to set a good example to the brethren.
And I am certain that, were my infirmity to leave me, the
greatest help that I could give the Order would be to pray
constantly to God for it, that He would govern, defend, and
preserve it.'

Now, as has already been mentioned, Saint Francis did his
best to conceal the most holy Stigmata, and ever since he had
received them he always went about with his feet shod and
his hands bandaged; but he could not prevent many friars

from seeing and touching them on various occasions, especially the wound in his side which he did his utmost to conceal. So a certain friar who was looking after him once cunningly persuaded him by a pious ruse to remove his habit so that he could shake out the dust; and when Saint Francis did so in his presence, the friar saw the wound in his side, and quickly resting his hand on his breast, he touched the wound with three fingers, and measured its width and length. And on a similar occasion it was seen by his Vicar.

Brother Ruffino, however, who was a great contemplative, received even clearer evidence. It was of him that Saint Francis said that there was no holier man than he in the whole world, and because of his sanctity he loved him with an intimate affection and granted whatsoever he desired. This Brother Ruffino assured himself and others in three ways about the Stigmata, and about the wound in the side in particular. The first way was this: having to wash Saint Francis's under-garment, which he wore large enough to be drawn up to cover the wound in the right side, Brother Ruffino examined it carefully, and each time he found it blood-stained on the right side. By this means he knew for certain that blood flowed from the wound, and Saint Francis reproached him when he realized that he had examined the garment to discover the blood. The second way was this: on one occasion Brother Ruffino intentionally touched Saint Francis's side, and moved his hand so as to place his fingers on the wound in his side. Saint Francis cried loudly at this, because of the intense pain he felt, saying, 'God forgive you, Brother Ruffino! Why did you do this?' The third way was this: Brother Ruffino once very earnestly begged Saint Francis as a great favour to give him his own cloak and take his own in exchange for love of charity. The loving father consented to this request, although with reluctance, and took off his own cloak, accepting the other in return; and during this exchange Brother Ruffino obtained a clear sight of the wound.

Similarly Brother Leo and many other friars saw these Stigmata of Saint Francis, and they may be believed because of their holiness, and their simple word is trustworthy. But, in order to remove all doubt from men's minds, they took an oath on the Holy Gospels that they had clearly seen them. Certain Cardinals, also, who were very well acquainted with him, saw them, and wrote fine hymns and composed antiphons and proses in honour of the sacred Stigmata of Saint Francis. Alexander, the Supreme Pontiff, preaching to a congregation that included all the Cardinals, among whom was the holy friar Bonaventura, himself a Cardinal, stated and affirmed that when Saint Francis had been alive, he had seen the holy Stigmata with his own eyes. The Lady Jacopa di Settesoli, who was the greatest Roman lady of her time, and was greatly devoted to Saint Francis, saw and kissed them with profound reverence on many occasions both before and after his death; for she came from Rome to Assisi by divine revelation at the time of Saint Francis's death, which took place as follows.

Some days before his death Saint Francis lay sick in the Bishop's palace at Assisi, attended by some of his companions, and despite his illness, he often sang the praises of Christ. One day one of his companions* said to him: 'Father, you know how the townspeople here have great trust in you and regard you as a holy man. They may think that, if you are what they believe you to be, you should be considering your death during this sickness, and weep rather than sing, because this illness of yours is serious. And remember that this singing of yours and ours in which you make us join is heard by many people in the palace and outside, for on your account this palace is guarded by many men-at-arms, who may receive a wrong impression. So I think,' said this friar, 'that you would do well to leave this place, and that we

---

* According to the *Mirror of Perfection* (Chapter 121), this friar was Brother Elias, the Minister General of the Order.

should all return to Saint Mary of the Angels, for we are not at home here among seculars.' Saint Francis replied: 'Dearest brother, you know that two years ago, when we were at Foligno, God revealed both to you and to me when my life would come to an end, and this end will come in a few days during this illness. And in the same revelation God assured me of the forgiveness of all my sins and of my entry into the blessedness of Paradise. Until that revelation I used to weep at the thought of my death and of my sins, but since I received that revelation I have been full of joy, so that I can weep no longer. That is why I sing, and will sing to God, who has given me the blessings of His grace and assured me of the glory of Paradise. As to our leaving here, I gladly agree; but you will have to find some means of carrying me, for my weakness will not permit me to walk.' Then the friars took him up in their arms and carried him, accompanied by many of the townspeople.

And when they reached an inn that stood by the roadside, Saint Francis said to those who were carrying him: 'Lay me down on the ground, and turn me so that I may face the city.' And when he had been placed with his face towards Assisi, he blessed it with many blessings, saying: 'May God bless you, sacred city, for many souls shall be saved through you, and many servants of God shall dwell in you; and from you many shall be chosen to the kingdom of everlasting life.' And when he had said these words, he was carried on to Saint Mary of the Angels. And on their arrival they carried him into the infirmary, and laid him down to rest.

Then Saint Francis called one of the companions and said to him: 'Dearest brother, God has revealed to me that in a few days I shall depart this life during this illness. You know the Lady Jacopa di Settesoli, who is a devout lover of our Order. Were she to hear of my death and not be present she would be very distressed. So send her word that if she wishes to see me alive, she must come at once.' The friar replied:

'Certainly, Father; in view of her great devotion to you, it would be most unseemly if she were not present at your death.'

'Go, then,' said Saint Francis, 'and bring writing materials, and write as I shall dictate.'

And when he had brought them, Saint Francis dictated the letter in this form:

To the Lady Jacopa, servant of God, Brother Francis, Christ's poor little one, sends greeting and the fellowship of the Holy Spirit in our Lord Jesus Christ.

Dearest Lady,

I wish you to know that Christ the Blessed has revealed to me by His grace that the end of my life is very near. So if you wish to find me alive, set out as soon as you have received this letter, and come to Saint Mary of the Angels; for if you have not arrived by a certain day at the latest, you will not find me alive. And bring with you sackcloth to shroud my body, and wax will be needed for my burial. I beg you, also, to bring some of that food* which you used to give me when I was ill in Rome.

And while this letter was being written, God revealed to Saint Francis that the Lady Jacopa was on her way to him, that she was already near the house, and that she had brought with her all the things for which he had asked in his letter. So, having received this revelation, Saint Francis told the friar who was writing that he need not continue since there was no need, but to put away the letter; at which, the friars were most surprised, for he had not finished the letter, nor did he want it despatched. After a short interval there was a loud knocking at the door, and Saint Francis sent the porter to open it; and when the door was opened, there stood Lady Jacopa, the noblest lady in Rome, with her two sons who were Senators, and a great company of horsemen. And when she came in,

---

* This sweetmeat, which Saint Francis enjoyed, seems to have been a speciality of Lady Jacopa's household, and was probably *frangipane*, an almond-flavoured delicacy.

the Lady Jacopa went straight to the infirmary to see Saint Francis. And Saint Francis was much pleased and comforted at her coming, and she was happy to see him alive and able to speak. Then she told him how God had revealed to her during prayer that his life was drawing to its close, and that he was about to send for her and ask for all those things that she had brought with her. And she had them brought in to Saint Francis, and she gave him something to eat.

When Saint Francis had eaten and was much refreshed, the Lady Jacopa knelt down and embraced his most holy feet which were sealed and adorned with the wounds of Christ. And with such devotion did she kiss them and bathe them with her tears that the friars standing round seemed to see the Madgalen herself at the feet of Jesus Christ, and were quite unable to draw her away. At length after a long while they raised her and took her aside; and they asked her how she had arrived provided with all things needed by Saint Francis, both now and at his death. The Lady Jacopa answered that while she was at prayer one night in Rome she heard a voice from heaven, which said to her: 'If you wish to find Saint Francis alive, go to Assisi without delay, and take with you such things as you usually give him when he is ill, and whatever is needed for his burial.' 'And this,' she said, 'I have done.'

And the Lady Jacopa remained there until Saint Francis passed from this life and was buried. And at his burial she and all her company paid him the highest honours, and bore the cost of all that was required. She then returned to Rome, and after a short time died a most holy death; and out of devotion to Saint Francis she directed that she should be carried to Saint Mary of the Angels and buried there. And it was done as she wished.

After the death of Saint Francis not only did the Lady Jacopa, with her sons and company, see and kiss the glorious Stigmata, but many others as well. Among these was a man named Jerome, who had doubts and was sceptical about them, just as Saint Thomas had doubted the wounds of Christ. In order to assure himself and others he boldly and publicly moved the nails in the hands and feet, and felt the wound in the side in the presence of friars and layfolk. As a result he became a firm witness, and testified on the Gospels that it was the truth, and that he had seen and touched them. Saint Clare and her nuns, who were present at Saint Francis's burial, also saw and kissed the glorious Stigmata.

Saint Francis, the glorious confessor of Christ, passed from this life in the year of our Lord 1226, on Saturday the third day of October, and was buried on the Sunday. This year was the twentieth after his conversion, when he began to do penance. He was canonized in the year 1228 by Pope Gregory IX, who visited Assisi in person to canonize him.

This concludes our fourth consideration of the glorious Stigmata of Saint Francis.

THE FIFTH CONSIDERATION: *Certain visions and revelations concerning the curious Stigmata*

THE fifth and last consideration concerns certain visions, revelations, and miracles which God showed and worked after the death of Saint Francis, in confirmation of his Stigmata and to establish the day and hour in which he received them from Christ.

On this subject it should be known that in the year of our Lord 1282 Brother Philip, Minister of Tuscany, under the instructions of Brother Buonagratia, the Minister General, required under holy obedience Brother Matteo of Castiglione Aretino, a very devout and holy man, to relate whatever he knew about the day and hour on which the sacred Stigmata were imprinted on the body of Saint Francis, since it had been said that he had received a revelation on the matter. Under the obligation of holy obedience, Brother Matteo replied as follows: While I was living in the community of La Verna last year during the month of May, I was at prayer one day in the cell which stands on the spot where it is believed that the appearance of the Seraph took place. And in my prayer I earnestly implored God that He would be pleased to reveal to someone the day, hour, and place in which the holy Stigmata were imprinted on the body of Saint Francis. And as I was continuing in prayer and persevering in this petition until after the first period of sleep, Saint Francis appeared in a brilliant light, and said to me: 'My son, what do you ask of God?'

'Father,' I replied, 'I am asking for such a thing.'

And he said to me: 'I am Francis, your Father: do you recognize me clearly?'

'I do, Father,' I said.

Then he showed me the Stigmata in his hands, and feet, and side, and said: 'The time has come when God wills to manifest to His glory those things that the friars have not hitherto tried to discover. Know, therefore, that He who appeared to me was not an angel, but Jesus Christ in the form of a Seraph. It was He who, with His own hands, imprinted on my body these five wounds, similar to those which He received in His own Body on the Cross. It happened in this way: the day before the Exaltation of the Cross an angel came to me, and told me in God's name to prepare myself by patience to receive that which God willed to send me. And I answered that I was ready to accept all things that it pleased God to send me.

The following morning, that is, the morning of Holy Cross Day, which that year fell on a Friday, I came out of my cell at dawn in very great fervour of spirit, and went to pray in the place where you now are, and where I often used to pray. And as I was praying, a young man crucified, in the form of a six-winged Seraph, swiftly descended through the sky from heaven. At His marvellous appearance I knelt humbly, and began to contemplate with devotion the boundless love of Jesus Crucified, and the infinite sorrow of His Passion. And His appearance caused so deep a compassion within me that it seemed as though I felt His Own Passion in my own body. At His presence this whole mountain shone like the sun, and He descended and drew near to me. And standing before me, He spoke to me certain secret words that I have hitherto revealed to no one; but the time is near when they shall be revealed. After a while Christ left me and returned to heaven, and later I found myself sealed with these wounds. 'Go, then,' said Saint Francis, 'and tell these things with assurance to your Minister, for this is the work of God, and not of man.' Having said this, Saint Francis gave me his blessing, and returned to heaven with a great host of young men in splendid robes.'

Brother Masseo stated that he had seen and heard all these things, not in a dream, but waking. And he testified to them in person before the Minister in his cell at Florence, when the latter required him to do so under obedience.

How for eight years a certain friar prayed God that he might learn the secret words spoken to Saint Francis when he received the Stigmata

On one occasion a certain devout and holy friar, while reading the chapter about the Stigmata in the Life of Saint Francis, began in great perplexity of spirit to wonder what these secret words might be which the Seraph had spoken to Saint Francis when He appeared to him, and which Saint Francis said that he would never reveal to anyone as long as he lived. And this friar said within himself: 'Saint Francis would never repeat these words during his lifetime; but now after his bodily death he might perhaps disclose them if he were asked devoutly.' And thenceforward this devout friar began to pray God and Saint Francis that they might be pleased to reveal them. And when the friar had persevered for eight years in this prayer, he was accounted worthy to receive an answer in the following way.

One day after the friars had dined and returned thanks in church, he remained to pray in another part of the church, and was calling on God and Saint Francis even more devoutly than usual and with many tears, when he was summoned by another friar and told on behalf of the Guardian to go with him to another place on the affairs of the house. So, not doubting that obedience is of greater merit than prayer, he interrupted his prayer immediately he received the order of his superior, and went out with the brother who had summoned him. And it pleased God that by this act of prompt obedience he was accounted worthy to receive the favour which he had failed to obtain by constant prayer. No sooner, therefore, were they outside the friary door than they met two unknown friars, who seemed to have come from some distant land; one of them appeared young, and the other old and thin, and they were both soaked and muddy because of the bad weather. So the obedient friar felt great compassion for them, and said to the companion with whom he was walking: 'Dearest brother, these unknown friars have great need of being charitably received; if the business on which we are travelling can be delayed a little, I beg you to let me first go and wash the feet of this older friar, who has the greater need, while you wash the feet of the younger. Afterwards we can set out on the affairs of the convent.'

When the other friar had assented to the charitable wish of his companion, they turned back and welcomed the unknown friars with all kindness. And they brought them to the kitchen fire to warm and dry themselves, where eight other friars belonging to the house were warming themselves.

When they had sat by the fire for a while, they took them aside to wash their feet, as they had agreed. And as the obedient and devout friar was washing the feet of the older friar and wiping away the mud – for they were very muddy – he saw that his feet were marked with the Stigmata; and he immediately embraced them with joy and wonder, crying: 'Either you are Christ, or you are Saint Francis!' At his cry and words the friars who were by the fire rose with great fear and reverence and hastened to look at these glorious Stigmata. Then at their entreaties the older friar allowed them to see them clearly, and to touch and kiss them. And while they were marvelling for joy, he said to them: 'Have no doubt, and do not be afraid, my beloved brothers and sons; I am your Father, Brother Francis, who by the will of God founded three Orders. And because during these past eight years I have been entreated by this friar who is washing my feet, and even more fervently today than at other times, that I would reveal to him those secret words which the Seraph spoke to me when He gave me the Stigmata, and which I would never disclose during my life, today by God's command and in reward for his willing obedience which moved him to forgo the sweetness of contemplation, I am commanded by God to reveal to you what he has asked.'

Then Saint Francis turned to this friar and spoke thus: 'Know, dearest brother, that while I was on Mount La Verna, wholly absorbed in the contemplation of Christ's Passion, during the vision of the Seraph I received the Stigmata in my body from Christ in this way. And afterwards Christ said to me: "Do you know what I have done to you? I have given you the marks of My Passion, so that you may be My Standard-Bearer. And as I descended into Limbo on the day of My death, and delivered all the souls that I found there by the merits of My Stigmata, and led them to Paradise, so do I grant you from this hour – in order that you may be conformed to Me in your death as you have been in your life – that after you have passed from this life, you shall go to Purgatory each year on the anniversary of your death, and by the virtue of these Stigmata I have given you, you shall deliver all the souls belonging to your three Orders, Minors, Sisters, and Penitents, together with those who have a special devotion to you, and you shall lead them to Paradise." And I did not disclose these words to anyone while I lived in this world.'

With these words Saint Francis and his companion suddenly vanished, and many friars later learned of these things from the eight friars who were present at this appearance and heard the words of Saint Francis.

A revelation is granted to Brother John

While Brother John of La Verna, a man of great holiness, was praying on Mount La Verna, Saint Francis appeared to him, and he remained and conversed with him for a considerable time. And at length, when he was about to leave him, Saint Francis said: 'Ask of me what you will.'

'Father,' replied Brother John, 'I beg you to tell me something that I have long desired to know. What you were doing and where you were when the Seraph appeared to you?'

Saint Francis replied: 'I was praying in the place where the chapel of Count Simon of Battifolle now stands, and I was asking two favours of my Lord Jesus Christ. The first was that, during my lifetime, He would allow me to feel in my soul and body, so far as is possible, the pain which He himself had felt at the time of His most bitter Passion. The second favour that I asked was similar, that I might feel in my heart that infinite love which moved Him to undergo such great suffering for us sinners. Then God put into my heart that He would grant both the one and the other, in so far as it were possible for a mere creature; and this promise was indeed fulfilled in me by the imprinting of the Stigmata.'

Then Brother John asked him whether those secret words which the Seraph had spoken to him were the same as those related by the above devout friar, who stated that he had heard them from Saint Francis in the presence of eight friars. Saint Francis replied that what the friar had said was true. Then Brother John took courage from Saint Francis's ready condescension, and said: 'Father, I earnestly beg you to allow me to see and kiss your glorious Stigmata, not that I have any doubts, but solely for my consolation, for I have always desired this favour.' And Saint Francis readily showed them and held them out to him, so that Brother John could see them clearly, touch, and kiss them.

Lastly Brother John asked: 'Father, what consolation did you feel within your soul when Christ the Blessed visited you and gave you the marks of His most sacred Passion? Would to God that I might feel a little of that sweetness!'

'Do you see these nails?' Saint Francis replied.

'Yes, Father,' replied Brother John.

'Touch this nail in my hand once more,' said Saint Francis.

Then with great reverence and fear Brother John touched the nail, and as soon as he had touched it, a great fragrance like a cloud of incense rose from it, and as it entered his nostrils it filled the soul and body of Brother John with such sweetness that he immediately entered into ecstasy and became insensible; and he remained rapt in God from that hour, which was the hour of Terce, until Vespers. And never until he came to die did Brother John speak of this vision and intimate conversation with Saint Francis except to his confessor; but when he was at the point of death, he disclosed it to a number of friars.

A revelation is granted to a holy and devout friar

A most devout and holy friar in the Province of Rome saw the following wonderful vision. A friar who was his dearest friend had died during the night, and was buried next morning at the entrance to the chapter-house. The same day this friar retired to a corner to pray devoutly to God and Saint Francis for the soul of his deceased companion. And as he persevered in his intercession with prayers and tears until noon, when all the other friars were asleep, he heard a great stir in the cloister. Moved to a sudden fear, he turned his eyes toward the tomb of his friend; and saw Saint Francis standing at the entrance to the chapter-house, and behind him a great company of friars all standing around the tomb. Looking beyond them, he saw a blazing fire in the centre of the cloister, and in the midst of the flames stood the soul of his dead friend: And gazing around the cloisters, he saw Jesus Christ walking along the cloister with a great company of angels and friars.

As he stared at these things with amazement, he saw that when Jesus Christ passed in front of the chapter-house, Saint Francis with all his friars knelt down, and said: 'I pray Thee, most holy Father and Lord, by that immeasurable charity which Thou didst show the human race in Thine Incarnation, that Thou wouldest have mercy on this my friar, who is burning in these flames.' And Christ made no reply, but passed on. And as Christ returned the second time and passed before the chapter-house, Saint Francis again knelt down with his friars as before, and prayed in these words: 'I pray Thee, compassionate Father and Lord, by that boundless charity which Thou didst show the human race when Thou didst die on the wood of the Cross, that Thou wouldest have mercy on this my friar.' And Christ again passed by, and gave no answer. And walking around the cloister, He returned the third time, and passed before the chapter-house; and then Saint Francis, kneeling as before, showed Him his hands and feet and breast, saying: 'I pray Thee, compassionate Father and Lord, by the great pain and great consolation which I felt when Thou didst imprint these holy Stigmata on my body, that Thou wouldest have mercy on the soul of my friar who is in this fire of Purgatory.' Wonderful to tell! As Christ was entreated the third time by Saint Francis in the name of his most holy and glorious Stigmata, He at once halted, and looking on the holy Stigmata, He granted his prayer, saying:

'Francis, I grant you the soul of your friar.' By so doing, He willed both to honour and confirm the glorious Stigmata of Saint Francis, and to testify openly that the souls of his friars who pass to Purgatory may be delivered from their pains and brought to the glory of Paradise by no easier way than through the merits of his Stigmata, in accordance with the words which Christ spoke to Saint Francis when He imprinted the sacred Stigmata.

No sooner had He uttered these words than the fire in the cloister died away, and the dead friar came to Saint Francis; and with him, and with Christ, and with their blessed company he ascended in glory to heaven. When his friend, the friar who had prayed for him, saw him delivered from his pains and taken to Paradise, he was filled with the greatest joy; and he told the whole vision to the other friars, and praised and thanked God with them.

How by God's command the devil testified to the holiness of Saint Francis and his holy Stigmata, and was then compelled to bear witness to the holiness of Saint Clare

A noble knight of Massa di San Pietro, named Landolfo, who was devoted to Saint Francis, and had at length received the habit of the Third Order from his own hands, was informed of the death of Saint Francis and of his glorious Stigmata in the following manner. When Saint Francis was nearing death, the devil entered into a woman living in that castle and cruelly tormented her; he also caused her to argue with such cunning that she confounded all the wise and scholarly men who came to reason with her. And it happened that the devil came out of her and left her free for two days; then, returning on the third day, he tormented her more cruelly than before. Hearing of this, Landolfo visited the woman and asked the devil who possessed her why he had left her for two days, only to return and torment her more fiercely than before.

The devil answered: 'When I left her, it was because I with all my confederates in these parts assembled together and went to the beggar Francis to dispute with him and seize his soul. But he was surrounded and guarded by a greater host of angels, and was carried by them direct to heaven. So we went away defeated, and now I have come back and repaid this wretched woman for what I had left undone those two days.'

Then Landolfo adjured him in God's name to tell the truth about the sanctity of Saint Francis, whom he reported to be dead, and about Saint Clare, who was living. The devil replied: 'Whether I wish it or not, I am speaking the truth. God the Father was so incensed at the sins of the world that it seems that in a short time He would pronounce His final sentence upon the men and women in it, and would have destroyed the world unless they repented. But Christ His Son, interceding for sinners, promised to renew His own life and Passion in a man, namely in Francis, the poor little beggar, through whose life and teaching He would recall many throughout the world to the ways of truth and penitence. And now, in order to show the world what He had done in Saint Francis, He willed that the Stigmata of His own Passion, which He had imprinted on his body during his life, should be seen and touched by witnesses after his death. The Mother of Christ likewise promised to renew her virginal purity and humility in a woman, namely in Sister Clare, in such a way that by her example she should deliver thousands of women out of our hands. Accordingly God the Father was appeased by these promises, and withheld His final judgement.'

Then Landolfo, wishing to learn for certain whether the devil, who is the father of lies, had spoken the truth in this matter, and especially as regards the death of Saint Francis, sent his trusted squire to Saint Mary of the Angels at Assisi to discover whether Saint Francis were alive or dead. And when the squire arrived, He found that it was as the devil had said;

and on returning to his master, he reported that Saint Francis had passed from this life on the very day and hour that the devil had said.

Pope Gregory publicly testifies to the holy Stigmata

Leaving aside all the miracles wrought through the Stigmata of Saint Francis, which may be read in his Life, it should be recorded at the conclusion of this fifth consideration that Pope Gregory IX had certain doubts about the wound in Saint Francis's side, as he later admitted. One night Saint Francis appeared to him, and raising his right arm a little, he showed him the wound in his side. Then Saint Francis asked for a flask, and when it had been brought, he caused it to be held beneath the wound in his side. And it seemed to the Pope that it was filled to the brim with blood mingled with water flowing from the wound; and from that moment all doubt vanished.

Later, in Council with all the Cardinals, he approved the Stigmata of Saint Francis, and in consideration of them granted the friars special privileges by a sealed bull. This he did at Viterbo in the eleventh year of his pontificate; then, during the twelfth year, he granted even further privileges. Later Pope Nicholas III and Pope Alexander granted abundant privileges, according to which anyone who denied the Stigmata might be proceeded against as a heretic.

And this concludes the fifth consideration of the glorious Stigmata of our Father Saint Francis. May God give us grace to imitate his life in this world, so that, by the virtue of these holy and glorious Stigmata, we may be found worthy of salvation and join him in Paradise.

TO THE PRAISE OF JESUS CHRIST AND OF
OUR MASTER SAINT FRANCIS

APPENDIX I

A SUMMARY OF EVENTS IN THE LIFE OF SAINT FRANCIS

1181 Born in Assisi of Pietro and Pica Bernadone.

1202 Francis is taken prisoner by the Perugians in a skirmish at Ponte San Giovanni, and remains in prison for a year.

1206 The crucifix of San Damiano bids Francis 'Repair My Church.' His conversion. He begins to rebuild San Damiano and S. Mary of the Angels (the Porziuncula).

1208 While at Mass in S. Mary of the Angels, S. Francis takes the words of the Gospel (Matthew 10) for his rule of life. He is soon afterwards joined by Bernard da Quintaville, Peter Catanii, and Giles.

1209 He travels to Rome, and obtains informal approval from Pope Innocent III on the Rule for the Friars Minor.

1211 The foundation of the Second Order of S. Francis. S. Clare receives the veil at the Porziuncula, and, after a period in the Benedictine Abbey of Sant'Angelo, is established at San Damiano.

1213 Count Orlando da Chiusi gives Mount La Verna to S. Francis as a place of retreat and prayer.

1215 The Lateran Council. The probable first meeting of S. Francis and S. Dominic.

1216 Pope Innocent III dies, and is succeeded by Pope Honorius III, who grants S. Francis the Porziuncula Indulgence.

1217 General Chapter of the Order at the Porziuncula. Foreign missions begun.

1219 Tension within the Order. S. Francis stands by his original Rule and ideals in the Chapter. He leaves with Peter Catanii and three other companions to visit the Crusading armies in Egypt, and is received by Sultan Melek-el-Kamil.

1220 S. Francis returns to Italy. Cardinal Ugolino becomes Protector of the Order. Francis resigns as Minister General, and is succeeded by Peter Catanii. S. Antony of Padua joins the Order.

1221 Death of Peter Catanii, who is succeeded by Brother Elias. Francis draws up a Rule in 23 chapters. The original Rule of the Third Order was probably drawn up in this year.

1223 Pope Honorius approves the Rule of 1223, to which Cardinal Ugolino had contributed much advice. S. Francis spends Christmas at Greccio, and makes the first Christmas crib.

A summary of events

1224 The first friars under B. Agnellus arrive in England, and establish themselves in Canterbury, London, and Oxford.

S. Francis travels to La Verna to observe a fast between the Feast of the Assumption and Michaelmas. On the Feast of the Exaltation of the Holy Cross he receives the Stigmata of Christ, and later returns to the Porziuncula.

1225 S. Francis, while gravely ill at San Damiano, composes the *Song of Brother Sun*.

1226 Unable to attend Chapter because of sickness, Francis writes his *Letter to the Chapter General and all the friars*. He dictates his *Testament*. Death of S. Francis at the Porziuncula on the evening of 3 October.

THE TESTAMENT OF SAINT FRANCIS

(dictated at Saint Mary of the Angels about
September 1226)

THE LORD granted me, Brother Francis, grace to begin to do penance, for while I was living in sin, it seemed a very bitter thing to look at lepers; but the Lord Himself led me among them, and I showed pity on them. And when I left them, the thing that had seemed so horrible to me was transformed into happiness of body and soul for me. After this I delayed awhile, and then renounced the world. And the Lord gave me such faith in His Church that I prayed to Him in simplicity and said: 'We adore Thee, O Lord Jesus Christ, here and in all Thy churches throughout the world, and we bless Thee, because by Thy holy Cross Thou hast redeemed the world.'

After this, the Lord gave me, and still gives me, such faith in priests who live according to the precepts of the holy Roman Church in respect of their Orders, that even were they to persecute me, I would wish to resort to them. And if I had as great wisdom as Solomon, and found very poor secular priests, I would not preach in their parishes without their consent. I desire to respect them and all others, and to love and honour them as my superiors; and I will not see any sin in them, because I see in them the Son of God, and look on them as my superiors. And I wish the most holy Sacrament to be honoured above all things, and venerated and reserved in precious places. And wherever I find writings containing God's most holy Name and word lying in unfitting places, I gather them together and put them in a seemly place. And we should honour and respect all theologians, and those who teach the most holy Word of God as those who minister spirit and life to us.

And after the Lord had given me brethren, no man showed me what to do; but the Most High Himself revealed to me how I must live in accordance with the precepts of the Holy Gospel. And I dictated a simple Rule in a few words, and the Lord Pope confirmed it for me. And those who came to embrace this way of life gave all that they had to the poor, and were content with a single habit, patched inside and out, and a cord and breeches. And we had no desire for anything more.

Those of us who were in Orders recited the Office like other clergy, while the lay-brethren said the *Our Father*. And we were content to live in abandoned churches, and to be looked on as ignorant and subject to all men. And I myself work with my hands, and wish to do so; and it is my firm intention that all other brothers should work in some honest occupation. Those who do not know a craft must learn, not in order to make a profit from their work, but to set a good example and to avoid idleness. And whenever we are not given our due wages for work, let us approach the Lord's table and seek alms from door to door.

The Lord has revealed to me that we should use this greeting: 'The Lord give you peace.' Let all the brethren beware of accepting churches, houses, or anything else provided for them unless they conform to Holy Poverty, to which we are vowed in our Rule, always lodging 'as strangers and pilgrims'.

Under holy obedience I strictly forbid all brethren, wherever they may be, to presume to solicit any letters [granting privileges] from the Court of Rome, either in person or through another, whether it be for a church, or other place, nor under the pretext that it is necessary for preaching or to avoid persecution. But wherever they are not received, let them go to another place and do penance with the blessing of God.

And I firmly intend to obey the Minister General of this Fraternity and any Guardian whom he is pleased to appoint over me. And I am content to be wholly in his hands, so that I cannot go anywhere or do anything contrary to obedience and to his will, since he is my superior. And although I am simple and infirm, I wish none the less always to have a priest to minister to me as is enjoined in the Rule.

And let all the other brethren be obliged to obey their Guardians, and to fulfil their obligations under the Rule. And if any are found who do not fulfil their obligations according to the Rule and wish to deviate from it, or who are not good Catholics, then all his other brethren, wherever they may be, are required under obedience to bring him to the nearest Guardian. And the Guardian is to keep him close like a man in chains day and night, so that he cannot escape from his custody until he hands him over personally to his own Minister. And the Minister is likewise required under obedience to keep him in charge of suitable brethren, who are to watch him day and night until they can bring him before the Lord Cardinal of Ostia, who is the master, protector, and corrector of this Fraternity.

And let not the brethren say, 'This is a new Rule', for it is a reminder, a warning, and an encouragement. It is my Testament, which I, little Brother Francis, make for you, my blessed brothers, with the intention

The Testament of Saint Francis

that as Catholics we may better obey the Rule which we have promised our Lord to obey.

And the Minister General and all other Ministers and Guardians are bound under obedience not to add or subtract anything from these words of mine. Let them keep this Testament always with them, together with the Rule, and at every Chapter that they summon, when they read the Rule, let them read these words as well.

And all my brethren, both clergy and lay-brothers, I firmly enjoin under obedience not to add glosses to the Rule or to these words, saying, 'It shall be understood thus'. But as our Lord has granted me to speak simply and clearly, and to write this Rule and these words simply and clearly, so shall you understand them simply and clearly, and observe them with holy deeds until the end.

And whosoever shall observe these things shall in heaven be filled with the blessing of our Father, the Most High, and on earth he shall be blessed by His beloved Son, and by the Holy Spirit the Paraclete, and by all the powers of heaven, and by all the saints.

And I, Brother Francis, your little servant, to the utmost of my power, confirm you inwardly and outwardly in this most holy blessing. *Amen.*

THE SONG OF BROTHER SUN

Mostly composed in the garden of Saint Clare's convent of San
Damiano in the summer of 1225 during Saint Francis's illness.
It has been described as 'the most beautiful
fragment of religious poetry
since the Gospels'.

Most High, Almighty, good Lord,
Thine be the praise, the glory, the honour,
And all blessing.

To Thee alone, Most High, are they due,
And no man is worthy
To speak Thy Name.

Praise to Thee, my Lord, for all Thy creatures,
Above all Brother Sun
Who brings us the day and lends us his light;

Lovely is he, radiant with great splendour,
And speaks to us of Thee,
O Most High.

Praise to Thee, my Lord, for Sister Moon and the stars
Which Thou hast set in the heavens,
Clear, precious, and fair.

Praise to Thee, my Lord, for Brother Wind,
For air and cloud, for calm and all weather,
By which Thou supportest life in all Thy creatures.

Praise to Thee, my Lord, for Sister Water,
Who is so useful and humble,
Precious and pure.

Praise to Thee, my Lord, for Brother Fire,
By whom Thou lightest the night;
He is lovely and pleasant, mighty, and strong.

Praise to Thee, my Lord, for our sister Mother Earth
Who sustains and directs us,
And brings forth varied fruits, and coloured flowers, and plants.

The Song of Brother Sun

*Praise to Thee, my Lord, for those who pardon one another
For love of Thee, and endure
Sickness and tribulation.

Blessed are they who shall endure it in peace,
For they shall be crowned by Thee,
O Most High.

†Praise to Thee, my Lord, for our Sister bodily Death
From whom no man living may escape:
Woe to those who die in mortal sin.

Blessed are they who are found in Thy most holy will,
For the second death cannot harm them.

Praise and bless my Lord,
Thank Him and serve Him
With great humility.

* This stanza was composed by Saint Francis to reconcile the Bishop
and Podestà of Assisi, who had been at enmity.
† This stanza was added by Saint Francis as he felt death approaching.

SAINT FRANCIS'S PARAPHRASE OF THE LORD'S PRAYER

OUR FATHER,

> most holy,
> Creator,
> Redeemer,
> Saviour,
> Comforter,

WHO ART IN HEAVEN,

> in the Angels and Saints
> enlightening them to knowledge of Thee,
> for Thou, Lord, art Light;
> inflaming them to love of Thee,
> for Thou, Lord, art Love;
> dwelling in them, and filling them with blessing,
> for Thou, Lord, art the highest good,
> the eternal good,
> from Whom all good proceeds,
> without Whom nothing is good.

HALLOWED BE THY NAME,

> may it be glorified in us
> by knowledge of Thee,
> that we may perceive
> the wideness of Thy blessings,
> the extent of Thy promises,
> the height of Thy majesty,
> the depth of Thy judgements.

THY KINGDOM COME,

> that Thou mayest reign in us
> by Thy grace,
> and bring us to Thy Kingdom,
> where the vision of Thee is revealed,
> and Thy love made perfect,
> that we may enter Thy blessed presence,
> and enjoy Thee for ever.

Paraphrase of the Lord's Prayer

THY WILL BE DONE IN EARTH AS IT IS IN HEAVEN,

that we may love Thee with all our heart,
ever thinking of Thee,
and desiring Thee with all our soul
and with all our mind;
directing all our intentions to Thee,
and seeking Thine honour in all things;
with all our strength
devoting every power and faculty
of mind and body to the service of Thy love,
and to no other end.
May we also love our neighbours as ourselves,
drawing them to love of Thee
with all our power;
delighting in the good of others
as in our own,
sharing in their troubles,
and giving no offence to any.

GIVE US THIS DAY OUR DAILY BREAD,

which is Thy beloved Son
Jesus Christ our Lord,
in the remembrance, understanding, and reverence
of the love that He bore us,
and for the things that He said, did, and endured
for our sakes.

AND FORGIVE US OUR TRESPASSES,

through Thine infinite mercy,
and by virtue of the Passion
of Thy beloved Son our Lord
Jesus Christ,
and through the merits and prayers
of the most blessed Virgin Mary
and of all Thine elect.

AS WE FORGIVE THEM THAT TRESPASS AGAINST US,

and since we do not forgive fully
do Thou, Lord, enable us to forgive fully
so that we may truly love our enemies
for Thy sake,

Paraphrase of the Lord's Prayer

and pray for them devoutly to Thee,
not returning evil for evil,
but seeking to serve all men in Thee.

AND LEAD US NOT INTO TEMPTATION,

hidden or open,
sudden or persistent,

BUT DELIVER US FROM EVIL,

past,
present,
and to come.

AMEN.

APPENDIX 5

SAINT FRANCIS'S BLESSING GIVEN TO BROTHER LEO*

THE Lord bless you and keep you. May He show you His face and be merciful to you. May He turn His countenance to you, and give you peace. The Lord bless you, Brother Leo. T [the sign *Tau*].

On the reverse is this Praise of God

THOU alone art holy, Lord God, who doest wondrous things. Thou art strong, Thou art great. Thou art the Most high. Thou art the Almighty King, the holy Father, King of heaven and earth. Thou art Trinity and Unity, O Lord God, all Goodness. Thou art Good, all Good, the Supreme Good, Lord God, living and true. Thou art Charity and Love. Thou art Wisdom. Thou art Humility. Thou art Patience. Thou art Serenity. Thou art Peace. Thou art Joy and Gladness. Thou art Justice and Temperance. Thou art our wealth, our treasure, and our satisfaction. Thou art Beauty. Thou art Clemency. Thou art our Protector. Thou art our Guardian and Defender. Thou art Strength. Thou art Refreshment. Thou art our Hope. Thou art our Trust. Thou art our great Delight. Thou art Eternal Life, great and wondrous Lord, Almighty God, merciful Saviour.

* The original is preserved at Assisi; and see the second Consideration, page 155.